W9-CCB-762

ONE-POT CAKES

ONE-POT

CAKES

60 Recipes for Cakes from Scratch
Using a Pot, a Spoon, and a Pan

ANDREW SCHLOSS WITH
KEN BOOKMAN

WILLIAM MORROW AND COMPANY, INC. • NEW YORK

Copyright © 1995 by Andrew Schloss and Ken Bookman

All rights reserved. No part of this book may be reproduced or utilized in any form or by any means, electronic or mechanical, including photocopying, recording, or by any information storage or retrieval system, without permission in writing from the Publisher. Inquiries should be addressed to Permissions Department, William Morrow and Company, Inc., 1350 Avenue of the Americas, New York, N.Y. 10019.

It is the policy of William Morrow and Company, Inc., and its imprints and affiliates, recognizing the importance of preserving what has been written, to print the books we publish on acid-free paper, and we exert our best efforts to that end.

Library of Congress Cataloging-in-Publication Data

Schloss, Andrew, 1951–
    One-pot cakes / by Andrew Schloss with Ken Bookman.
      p.   cm.
    ISBN 0–688–14138–2
    1. Cake. 2. Quick and easy cookery. I. Bookman, Ken.
    II. Title.
    TX771.S26   1995
    641.8'653—dc20   94–42177   CIP

Printed in the United States of America

First Edition

ILLUSTRATIONS BY DOROTHY REINHARDT

BOOK DESIGN BY JESSICA SHATAN

To Joan Horn,
for refusing to spend any more time
in the kitchen than is absolutely necessary.

ACKNOWLEDGMENTS

We would like to offer our heartfelt thanks to the many people who have contributed to this, our third cookbook, and whose support has been important to all our book work.

To Judith Weber, our persistent agent, who blessed this project from the start and gave it constant support and invaluable critiques.

To Harriet Bell, our editor at Morrow, for seeing the importance of this little book and giving it a life much fuller than we ever anticipated.

To Susan Derecskey, our copyeditor, who has, once again, confined egg to our recipes and kept it off our faces.

To Jessica Shatan, a master book builder, who wrapped this humble manuscript in a perfectly beautiful package.

To Dorothy Reinhardt, whose unique drawing style gave this book great fun and elegance.

And to Lisa and Lou Ekus for their support and guidance for all our projects.

—ANDREW SCHLOSS AND KEN BOOKMAN

You, like my friends, may want to know exactly who Ken Bookman, my book partner, is, and what he does for his "with" status on the covers of our books. Well, it's like this. I live in a confined world of word and food processing and like most chefs love food so much that I often lose sight of a larger world that does not instantly grasp the inherent attraction between liver and raspberries. Ken never loses sight of that world. Not only does he edit the text I write, edit the recipes I invent, and test some of the recipes, too, but he challenges my assumptions and approach to things and removes the culinary excesses, purple phrases, and misspellings that my work is prone to. Ken is my thought processor, and to him I am forever indebted.

And thanks, also:

To Adele Zipser, for having a cake this easy in her cooking repertoire.

To the Horn clan, Burt, Joan, Abby, Zach, Max, Nomi, and Alice, who tasted, tested, inspired, and critiqued.

To the Aions, for being self-indulgent enough to relish any dinner that began and ended with cake.

To the Schecter, Keidan, Jacobson, Shaye, Wohl, and Schneider families, for spending a weekend planning each activity around a rigorous schedule of eating cake.

To Karen Shain Schloss, who survived the temptation of this book without complaint.

To Dana, Ben, and Isaac, my much loved and very picky children, who managed to taste and test Cassis Torte with the same vigor as Chocolate Chocolate-Chip Bars.

—A.S.

Andrew Schloss and I have worked together for about thirteen years now. He is the creative genius behind the three books we've produced together—inventing, writing, and in many cases testing the recipes around which the books are built, and constantly finding new ways to teach cooking to the rest of the world. His talent as a food man is extraordinary and the friendship that has developed between us is an important part of my life. What may surprise many people, even him, is how he has made me a better editor. The better authors are the only ones who can do that, and Andy's work is so good and so conscientious that I'd be embarrassed to even think of editing it unless I was at the top of my game. He has my utmost gratitude for making these years so rewarding.

This is also the third book I've done while sharing a home with Ruth Adelman, and it's the second one where she has never known when she might return home to find hot and cold running cakes all over the place. It is not an easy way to live, and her grace, humor, and love have helped immensely. In return, she already has my love; I hope the grace and humor can be repaid in due course.

Many friends and family members have been extraordinary sources of support through the many difficult times that books can entail, and I'm deeply grateful to all of them. A few, including Don Bookman, Jack Bookman, Thelma Bookman, David Corcoran, Morrie Goldfischer, Bob Greenberg, Cathy Guisewite, Carol Horner, Rick Nichols, and Liz Williams, have been especially beneficial to my mental health.

—K.B.

CONTENTS

INTRODUCTION

I have done the impossible. In four months of testing and retesting sev-enty cake and icing recipes, not once have I turned on a mixer, picked up a sifter, or separated an egg. I am still on the same economy-size squeeze bottle of dishwashing detergent I bought at the beginning of the project, and far from being fed up with cakes and cake baking, I can't wait to get back into the kitchen and see what new recipes I can simplify with the easy one-pot baking method that is the subject of this book.

In this volume are more cake recipes than you should ever need, and not one of them requires more than a mixing bowl, a utensil or two, a baking pan, and something to measure with. The process is so simple and so fast that it has changed forever my notion of cake making.

The prospect of baking a cake had always seemed like a big deal to me. I gladly did it for special occasions. But for an everyday dessert? No way! Not only did it require advance planning to soften butter, for example, but it meant hauling out and cleaning up an arsenal of strainers, spatulas, beaters, and bowls.

Joan's recipe changed all that.

I have known Joan, her family, and her chocolate cake for more than a baker's dozen of years. When our families gathered for a Sunday dinner, there was never a question about Joan's contribution. Every time I dropped in, there was a chocolate cake either on the counter, going into the oven, or coming out of the oven. The cakes were good, but the wonder of them was that they were produced so regularly by someone who was otherwise culinarily impaired.

When I asked Joan about where she got her baking stamina, she answered by handing me the recipe and explaining that if it took me longer than ten minutes to put the ingredients together, I had done something wrong.

Sure enough, this cake was a nonbaker's dream. Fewer than ten ingredients. No sifting, no creaming, no beating, no whipping. You just threw everything together and slid it in the oven. And best of all, the cleanup was a snap—one pot, one spoon, one pan.

Soon, I, too, had chocolate cakes cascading across the counter, and as I applied this simple method to other cakes, I had piles of butter cakes, coffee cakes, carrot cakes, cheesecakes, and brownies as well, all vying for storage space in the freezer.

Here are the particulars.

The One-Pot Method

Traditionally, cake recipes begin by beating softened butter with sugar until the mixture is very thick and aerated. Into this mixture are blended eggs, sometimes beaten egg whites, flavored extracts, milk, and sifted dry ingredients.

The one-pot method streamlines the process.

First, creaming the butter and sugar is replaced by something far simpler: The butter is half melted in a large saucepan then stirred off the stove, so its residual heat completes the melting. If chocolate is part of the recipe, it's added off the heat, where the butter's warmth melts it without danger of scorching. During that time, the mixture cools sufficiently so that when the eggs are added, they don't curdle in hot butter.

To further ensure that the mixture has cooled before the eggs go in, less heat-sensitive ingredients—sugar, vanilla, spices, sour cream, or yogurt—are added first. Then the eggs are added, followed by the dry ingredients.

Another traditional step that's streamlined away in the one-pot method is the sifting of dry ingredients. There's only one reason to sift flour, and that's to aerate it. But aerating flour is essential only for the most delicate sponge or angel food cakes. Many cooks believe that sifting is necessary to blend dry ingredients before they are added to the batter. This makes sense —until you observe what actually happens during sifting. It's most obvious when you sift dark and light ingredients together, flour and cocoa powder, for instance. Watch what happens: The cocoa stays pretty much in the same small area where it started. It isn't distributed thoroughly until the dry ingredients are mixed into the batter.

The two ingredients in cake recipes that are prone to lumping are baking powder and baking soda. The one-pot method addresses that, too, in a simple way: Add those ingredients in pinches. That way, using your fingers, you can break up any lumps before they go into the batter. Baking powder and soda are also added to the batter before the flour, so they can soften and disperse through the liquid before more dry ingredients get in the way.

And in several small ways, such as breaking chocolate with your fingers and adding bananas whole, you avoid having to use and wash an extra utensil. In most cases, the batter is mixed with a plain wooden spoon. Batter should not become lumpy, but if one ever does, use a stiff whisk or a serving fork to break up the lumps.

The one-pot method gives you the quality of a cake made from scratch with the convenience of a mix—and with less cleanup. I think you'll find the results exceptional, considering the small outlay of time and the minute neffort that these recipes require. Doubtless, there are some elaborate professional-quality cakes that could never be distilled down to one-pot preparations. This book makes no claim to revolutionize the art of the pastry chef but it just might reinvent cake making in your home, transforming an arduous specialty into an everyday pleasure.

About the Ingredients

With only a couple of exceptions, all the ingredients for these cakes should be available in any well-stocked supermarket. A small number of ingredients, such as dried cherries, may require a visit to a specialty market. Here are a few specific notes about ingredients:

Butter. I use only unsalted butter. The salt content among different brands of salted butter varies so greatly that it's impossible to predict the flavor of a cake in which salted butter is used.

Buttermilk. The acidic nature of buttermilk is essential to the texture of many cakes. If you don't have any and would rather not buy an entire quart, you can substitute the same quantity of a 50–50 mixture of either plain yogurt and milk or sour cream and milk.

Canned fruits and fillings. Many of the recipes call for a fruit or nut filling. For the most part, they are sold in cans containing 12 or 12½ ounces, and the recipes are written to use that measurement. I did, however, find one manufacturer whose products came in 10-ounce jars. If that's all you can buy, there's no need to buy an extra jar. Use the contents of one jar. The missing ounces, which amount to only a tablespoon or two, will not affect the finished product.

Chocolate. The chocolates I use are Baker's, Nestlé, or Hershey's.

Cocoa. Cocoa is unsweetened, defatted chocolate powder. Most of the cakes that use cocoa were tested with Hershey's Cocoa, although any brand will give you similar results. If you use Dutch- or European-processed cocoa, expect the cake to be much darker.

Coffee and tea. When a cake calls for instant-coffee powder, use any brand. Freeze-dried coffee is fine. One recipe, Maple Banana Cake, calls for tea. The pre-brewed bottled tea specified in the recipe saves you from using an additional vessel, but you can also brew a cup of tea using any standard tea bag.

Dried citrus peel. Minced dried lemon and orange peels are sold in the spice section of many supermarkets or in specialty stores. Using them will save you labor and cleanup, but freshly grated or minced citrus zest can be substituted for the dried product without adjusting measurement.

Dried fruit. Several of the recipes call for dried fruits, including raisins (both golden and dark), currants, cherries, and mixed diced fruit. The only one you might not find at your supermarket are dried cherries; these are available in gourmet food stores and many health-food stores, and they are well worth seeking out. Look for dried sour (or red) cherries for the best flavor.

Eggs. The cakes were tested with both large and extra-large eggs and either size is fine.

Flour. All-purpose flour was used in testing, and either bleached or unbleached is fine. Whole wheat flour is used in a couple of recipes.

Milk. Use any milk you have on hand. Fat content will not affect these recipes.

Nuts. The nuts specified in these recipes are varieties available already ground so you can avoid using another piece of kitchen equipment. In fact, many other nut varieties work perfectly well in these recipes. If you don't mind the extra time and cleanup of grinding them yourself, go ahead and use them.

Sour cream. Either regular or reduced-fat sour cream can be used, but nonfat sour cream will not work in baking.

Vegetable oil sprays. These sprays (Pam is a common brand) make a two-second task out of greasing a cake pan.

Yogurt. These recipes were tested with lowfat yogurt, but any yogurt will work.

About the Techniques

Grinding nuts. I call for preground nuts to help minimize cleanup, but if you have a food processor and an extra minute or two, grinding nuts yourself is a snap. Measure about 25 percent more nut pieces than the volume of ground nuts that the recipe calls for (if using a weight measure, the measurement stays the same). Use the pulse button of your processor in two or three bursts of no more than five seconds' duration to coarsely chop the nuts. Continue pulsing in shorter bursts until the nuts are uniformly ground into a powder as fine as sand. The object is to get the nuts as fine as possible without transforming them into nut butter. So if they begin to clump or look oily, stop and use them as they are.

Mashing bananas. When a batter has bananas in it, the fruit should be very ripe to ensure a better-tasting cake and allow the bananas to be easily mashed with the back of a serving fork. Don't worry about leaving a few small lumps. Like chocolate chips and raisins, a few banana chunks will add flavor and texture.

Melting butter and chocolate. In recipes that call for melting butter and/or chocolate, use a heavy-bottomed, 3-quart saucepan for mixing the batter. Begin melting butter over a flame, but finish the melting off the flame, letting the residual heat finish the job. When a recipe asks for melted chocolate, use your hand to break the chocolate into pieces and add the pieces after the butter has melted about halfway. The melted butter protects the chocolate from scorching, so you may keep the chocolate over the flame until it is about half melted. Then allow the residual heat to finish the melting.

Pinching baking powder and soda. To avoid any lumping, measure them into your hand and pinch them with your fingers to break up any lumps before you add them to a batter. Add baking soda and powder to the batter before the flour. Stir well, but don't concern yourself with a few streaks. These will be disappear when you stir in the flour.

About the Baking Pans

In recipes that call for melting butter and/or chocolate, use a heavy-bottomed, 3-quart saucepan for mixing the batter. It doesn't matter what type of metal the saucepan is made of. In recipes that don't require melting, use that same saucepan or a large mixing bowl.

Although the types of cakes included in these pages vary widely, I've limited baking pans to those in a typical home kitchen. These are the baking pans used for the cakes in this book:

- 8-inch layer pan
- 9-inch square baking pan
- 2-quart casserole (soufflé dish) or 9-inch cheesecake pan
- 9-inch loaf pan
- 9-inch springform
- 10-inch tube pan
- 10-inch bundt pan
- 9 × 13 × 2-inch baking pan
- 10 × 15 × 1-inch jelly-roll pan
- 12-cup standard muffin tin

Most of the cakes are made in the 8-inch round pan. I think that pan yields a more attractive single layer than a 9-inch pan, which is why the recipes don't specify both. But if all you have is a 9-inch round pan, use it instead of the 8-inch pan and start checking the cake for doneness about five minutes sooner than the recipe says.

Some of the coffee cakes call for a 9-inch square baking pan, a 10-inch bundt or tube pan, or a standard 9-inch loaf pan. All the cupcakes are baked in a standard 12-cup nonstick muffin tin where each cupcake cup has a capacity of ½ cup and a top diameter of 3 inches. The sheet cakes use either a 9- × 13-inch baking pan or a 10- × 15-inch jelly-roll pan. Cheesecakes are baked in a 9-inch cheesecake pan or a 2-quart soufflé dish. One of the flourless cakes calls for a 9-inch springform pan.

One of the most talked about variables in baking is the color of the pan. I don't consider it as crucial as you may have been led to believe. Both glass and dark-colored metal absorb heat faster than shiny metal pans. But far more important are your oven's temperature and the likelihood that it has some hot and cold spots. If you've noticed that some of your baking pans transfer heat faster than others, lower your oven heat by 25 degrees when using those pans.

Some cakes are extra prone to sticking to the pan, and greasing (such as with vegetable oil spray) can eliminate that problem. Pans that are greased are frequently floured, too, for the same reason. After greasing, toss a small amount of flour into the pan and shake and rotate the pan until the flour adheres in a light, even coating. Toss out any excess flour and the pan is ready to receive batter.

Cakes that have a tendency to stick, like tortes, benefit from lining the cake pan with wax paper or kitchen parchment. To trim a sheet of wax paper to the size of a round cake pan, set the pan on the paper and trace a circle. Cut inside the line and trim a little more if necessary to fit the paper inside the pan.

To remove a cake from its pan, allow it to cool in the pan for about ten minutes. In that time, the cake will become a little sturdier and will release from the pan without cracking. Run a small, sharp knife around the edge of the cake to loosen it. Then cover the cake with wax paper, top with a rack or a large flat plate, and invert. The cake will fall from the pan. Remove the pan, cover with a cooling rack, and invert again. Remove the top rack or plate and paper, and cool for about fifteen more minutes.

Very soft cakes, such as cheesecakes, need extra help. Don't use a knife. Rather, loosen the edge by holding the warm pan on its side and let gravity pull the cake down. Rotate the pan a quarter turn and let the cake drop again. Keep turning until the cake has been released all around.

If the cake won't come out of the pan, shake the inverted pan vigorously from side to side. If the cake still won't come out, sharply rap the pan and its covering plate on the countertop to break any sticky spots across the bottom of the cake. If it still won't come out, turn it right side up and loosen the edge again with a knife, but this time push the edge of the cake away from the side of the pan with the blade of the knife. Invert again.

If it still won't come out, it's time to move on. Slice the cake right in the pan and lift out the pieces with a flexible spatula.

ONE-POT CAKES

CHOCOLATE CAKES

Chocolate Applesauce Cake

Chocolate Raspberry Cake

Chocolate Banana Cake

Devil's Food Cake

Double Chocolate Cake

Chocolate Fudge Cake

Chocolate Brandy Pudding Cake

Chocolate Bourbon Pecan Loaf

Pruny Chocolate Cake

Chocolate Pumpkin Spice Cake

Even though fat has become Public Enemy No. 1, chocolate remains the only ingredient for which fat-fearing Americans are willing to risk imagined doom. How else can one explain the current rash of morbid chocolate monikers? Otherwise fastidious dieters long for a Chocolate Death or a Cocoa Coronary.

Although adding chocolate is an effortless way to bake in richness, working with it has its quirks. First, there's melting. Chocolate burns easily, which is why most cookbooks warn against melting chocolate without the protection of a double boiler or a microwave. I go them one better: I finish melting the chocolate off the stove and right in the pot in which the batter will be mixed.

Most of the following cakes start by adding chocolate to hot melting butter and stirring so the residual heat from the butter helps melt the chocolate. That avoids any chance of burning the chocolate while at the same time cooling the butter so it won't scramble the eggs in the batter.

Once it's melted, chocolate can become grainy if it's mixed with water or anything containing water, such as an egg or a liquid flavoring. The one-pot method guards against this mishap, too. Chocolate is an emulsion of liquid (chocolate liquor) in fat (cocoa butter). Any additional liquid breaks the emulsion, leaving behind grains of chocolate in a sea of melted fat. Because these one-pot cakes start by melting chocolate with butter, extra liquid can easily be absorbed without fear of breaking the emulsion.

Chocolate comes in several forms. The main distinction between them is sweetening. Unsweetened chocolate is bitter, very dark, and quite brittle. Taken out of hand, it is inedible, but in baking it packs the biggest chocolate punch per pound. The principal brands are Baker's, Nestlé, and Hershey's.

Partially sweetened chocolates can be called bittersweet or semisweet, depending on the manufacturer. They vary in flavor and sweetness but generally have about half the amount of chocolate solids as unsweetened chocolate and four-tenths of an ounce of sugar added for every ounce of chocolate.

Fully sweetened chocolates are called sweet chocolate (if they are dark) or milk chocolate (if they are light).

Cocoa powder is unsweetened chocolate that has had about 75 percent of its fat removed. In a cake, it produces a darker and more chocolatey-tasting product. European cocoas are Dutch-processed, as is Hershey's European Style Cocoa. This means the chocolate is treated with a mild alkali, which causes the cocoa to become richer and darker and to mix more easily in liquid. Although I prefer Dutch-processed cocoa for making hot chocolate, I find it tastes flat in baking unless it's in a batter with other, more acidic ingredients, as in the Chocolate Pumpkin Spice Cake.

Chocolate Applesauce Cake

The idea that led to this book came from a friend who seemed to have an unending supply of chocolate cakes coming from her oven. After I marveled at her enterprise, she gave me this recipe to show me how little effort she actually gave the cakes. My friend stole it from her mother, who stole it from her neighbor, who stole it from an aunt, who has no idea that I've stolen it for you.

¼ pound (1 stick) unsalted butter

2 ounces unsweetened chocolate, broken into pieces

1¼ cups applesauce

1 cup sugar

Pinch of salt

1 tablespoon instant-coffee powder

1 teaspoon vanilla extract

2 eggs

½ teaspoon baking soda

1 cup flour

Preheat the oven to 350° F. Grease and flour an 8-inch layer pan.

In a large heavy saucepan over medium heat, begin melting the butter. When it's half melted, stir in the chocolate, remove from the heat when the chocolate is half melted, and stir until the butter and chocolate are fully melted.

Stir in the applesauce, sugar, salt, coffee powder, vanilla, and eggs. Add the baking soda in pinches, breaking up any lumps with your fingers. Stir in thoroughly. Stir in the flour, just until the mixture is blended.

Pour and scrape the batter into the pan and bake for 50 minutes, or until a tester inserted in the center comes out clean. Cool in the pan on a rack for 10 minutes. Remove from the pan and cool on the rack for about 15 minutes more.

Makes 6 to 8 servings

Chocolate Raspberry Cake

Is there anything better than the pairing of raspberry and dark chocolate? The two seem meant for each other, creating a tart-fruity-bitter-rich-sweet gestalt greater than the sum of its parts. This recipe calls for a can of raspberry pastry filling, which is usually sold in the baking section of supermarkets. If you prefer, use the same amount of seedless raspberry jam instead of raspberry filling, but reduce the amount of sugar to 2/3 cup.

¼ pound (1 stick) unsalted butter

2 ounces unsweetened chocolate, broken into pieces

1 can (12 ounces) raspberry filling

1 cup sugar

Pinch of salt

1 tablespoon vanilla extract

2 eggs

½ teaspoon baking soda

1 cup flour

Preheat the oven to 350° F. Grease and flour an 8-inch layer pan.

In a large heavy saucepan over medium heat, begin melting the butter. When it's half melted, stir in the chocolate. Remove from the heat when the chocolate is half melted, and stir until the butter and chocolate are fully melted.

Stir in the raspberry filling, sugar, salt, vanilla, and eggs. Add the baking soda in pinches, breaking up any lumps with your fingers. Stir in thoroughly. Stir in the flour, just until the mixture is blended.

Pour and scrape the batter into the pan and bake for 50 minutes, or until a tester inserted in the center comes out clean. Cool in the pan on a rack for 10 minutes. Remove from the pan and cool on the rack for about 15 minutes more.

Makes 6 to 8 servings

Chocolate Banana Cake

Not only do bananas lend flavor to this cake, but they give it a soft, creamy finish, delivering the punch of dark chocolate in a silken pillow of banana bread. It's a knockout.

¼ pound (1 stick) unsalted butter
2 ounces unsweetened chocolate, broken
   into pieces
2 very ripe bananas
1 cup sugar

Pinch of salt
1 teaspoon vanilla extract
2 eggs
½ teaspoon baking soda
1 cup flour

Preheat the oven to 350° F. Grease and flour an 8-inch layer pan.

In a large heavy saucepan over medium heat, begin melting the butter. When it's half melted, stir in the chocolate. Remove from the heat when the chocolate is half melted, and stir until the butter and chocolate are fully melted.

Add the bananas and mash with the back of a fork until almost incorporated. Stir in the sugar, salt, vanilla, and eggs. Add the baking soda in pinches, breaking up any lumps with your fingers. Stir in thoroughly. Stir in the flour, just until mixture is blended.

Pour and scrape the batter into the pan and bake for 45 minutes, or until a tester inserted in the center comes out clean. Cool in the pan on a rack for 10 minutes. Remove from the pan and cool on the rack for about 15 minutes more.

Makes 6 to 8 servings

Devil's Food Cake

Forget the bickerings of the recipe police. There is no genuine recipe for Devil's Food Cake. Rather, the name is a turn-of-the-century pun hinting at the sinful nature of chocolate compared to the lofty purity of an angel food cake. Devil's Food Cake is nothing more than a generic name for any rich chocolate cake. This one has the fine crumb of a cake that has been beaten for several minutes and the intensity of a batter pumped up with chocolate.

6 tablespoons (¾ stick) unsalted butter
2 ounces unsweetened chocolate, broken
   into pieces
1¼ cups (packed) dark brown sugar
1 teaspoon vanilla extract

Pinch of salt
2 eggs
1 teaspoon baking soda
1¼ cups flour
½ cup very hot water

Preheat the oven to 350° F. Grease and flour an 8-inch layer pan.

In a large heavy saucepan over medium heat, begin melting the butter. When it's half melted, stir in the chocolate. Remove from the heat when the chocolate is half melted, and stir until the butter and chocolate are fully melted.

Stir in the brown sugar, vanilla, salt, and eggs. Add the baking soda in pinches, breaking up any lumps with your fingers. Stir thoroughly. Stir in the flour, just until mixture is well blended. Stir in the water.

Pour and scrape the batter into the pan and bake for 20 to 25 minutes, or until the cake is springy and pulls away slightly from the sides of the pan. Cool on a rack for 10 minutes. Remove from the pan and cool on the rack for about 15 minutes.

Makes 12 servings

NOTE: For a great birthday cake, double the recipe, bake in 2 layers, and assemble with a double recipe of Chocolate Sour Cream Icing (page 97).

Double Chocolate Cake

The intense chocolate in this cake comes from two fronts. Semisweet chocolate is melted with butter to form a smooth chocolate base, and that base is darkened and enriched with cocoa powder. Cocoa, nothing more than concentrated chocolate, gives an extra chocolate boost without adding liquid or much more fat. Invariably, the darkest chocolate cakes use some, and sometimes all, cocoa to attain their deep color and flavor.

¼ pound (1 stick) unsalted butter

2 ounces semisweet chocolate, broken into pieces

1 cup sugar

¼ cup cocoa powder

Pinch of salt

1¼ cups applesauce

2 eggs

1 teaspoon baking soda

1¼ cups flour

Preheat the oven to 350° F. Grease and flour an 8-inch layer pan.

In a large heavy saucepan over medium heat, begin melting the butter. When it's half melted, stir in the chocolate. Remove from the heat when the chocolate is half melted, and stir until the butter and chocolate are fully melted.

Stir in the sugar, cocoa powder, salt, applesauce, and eggs. Add the baking soda in pinches, breaking up any lumps with your fingers. Stir in thoroughly. Stir in the flour, just until mixture is blended.

Pour and scrape the batter into the pan and bake for 50 minutes, or until a tester inserted in the center comes out clean. Cool in the pan on a rack for 10 minutes. Remove from the pan and cool on the rack for about 15 minutes more.

Makes 6 to 8 servings

Chocolate Fudge Cake

A box of chocolate-pudding mix is the secret behind this super-moist cake. In fact, it is so overwrought with chocolate that it's hard to know whether the finished product is more cake or confection.

¼ pound (1 stick) unsalted butter
6 ounces semisweet chocolate chips
1 cup sugar
1 cup whole, lowfat, or skim milk
1 box (about 4 ounces) instant chocolate
    pudding and pie filling

Pinch of salt
2 eggs
1 teaspoon baking soda
1¼ cups flour

Preheat the oven to 350° F. Grease and flour an 8-inch layer pan.

In a large heavy saucepan over medium heat, begin melting the butter. When it's half melted, stir in half the chocolate chips. When the chocolate is half melted, remove from the heat and stir until the butter and chocolate are fully melted.

Stir in the sugar, milk, pudding mix, salt, and eggs. Add the baking soda in pinches, breaking up any lumps with your fingers. Stir in thoroughly. Stir in the flour, just until mixture is blended. Stir in the rest of the chocolate chips.

Pour and scrape the batter into the pan and bake for 1 hour, or until a tester inserted in the center comes out slightly tacky. Cool in the pan on a rack for 10 minutes. Remove from the pan and cool on the rack for about 15 minutes.

Makes 6 to 8 servings

NOTE: If you wish, coat this cake with Chocolate Sour Cream Icing (page 97), any of the cream-cheese icings (pages 97–99), or, for complete decadence, Chocolate Mint Icing (page 99).

Chocolate Brandy Pudding Cake

Pudding cakes are a definitively American, decidedly homey dessert, in which a cake batter is topped with some sort of syrup and then baked. In the alchemy of the oven, the cake part rises up through the syrup. Or maybe it's the syrup that sinks down through the cake. At any rate, the exchange produces a moist brownie-like cake that rests on a swamp of chocolate pudding. To serve it, you scoop up some cake with its pudding and eat it with a spoon.

1 cup flour
2 teaspoons baking powder
½ teaspoon baking soda
¼ teaspoon salt
Pinch of cinnamon
1 cup sugar
½ cup cocoa powder

½ cup whole, lowfat, or skim milk
1 teaspoon vanilla extract
¼ cup vegetable oil
½ cup (packed) dark brown sugar
¼ cup brandy
¾ cup very hot water

Preheat the oven to 350° F. Grease a 9-inch square baking pan.

In a large mixing bowl, combine the flour, baking powder, baking soda, salt, cinnamon, ¾ cup of the sugar, and half the cocoa. Add the milk, vanilla, and oil and mix into a thick batter.

Spread the batter evenly in the pan. Sprinkle the top with the brown sugar, the remaining cocoa, and the remaining granulated sugar. Pour the brandy and hot water over the top. Bake for 30 minutes, or until the cake sets around the sides and the top is very loose and bubbly. Cool in the pan on a rack for 10 minutes or more. Slice or scoop to serve.

Makes 8 servings

Chocolate Bourbon Pecan Loaf

This cake, loaded with pecans, nut pastry filling, and a hefty shot of bourbon, is reminiscent of a classic Southern nut cake. The one shift is the addition of chocolate, which turns the recipe from a nut cake into a sort of chocolate pâté. Dense, moist, and rich, it is irresistible when served in thin slices with coffee or tea. And it's moist enough to make icing superfluous.

¼ pound (1 stick) unsalted butter
1 can (12 ounces) pecan filling
1 cup sugar
1 tablespoon vanilla extract
3 tablespoons bourbon
2 eggs

⅔ cup buttermilk
2 teaspoons baking soda
¼ teaspoon salt
½ cup cocoa powder
1½ cups flour
1 cup chopped pecans

Preheat the oven to 350° F. Grease a 9-inch loaf pan.

In a large heavy saucepan over medium heat, melt the butter. Remove from the heat.

Add in the pecan filling, stirring until smooth. Mix in the sugar, vanilla, bourbon, eggs, and buttermilk, stirring until smooth. Add the baking soda in pinches, breaking up any lumps with your fingers. Stir in thoroughly. Stir in the salt and cocoa. Stir in the flour, just until blended. Stir in the pecans.

Pour and scrape the batter into the pan and smooth the top. Bake for 1 hour, or until a tester inserted into the crack in the cake comes out clean. Cool in the pan on a rack for 10 minutes. Remove from the pan and cool on the rack for about 15 minutes more.

Makes 8 servings

Pruny Chocolate Cake

I am a great prune fan and an even greater fan of the prune-chocolate combination. To my palate, there is nothing quite so opulent. But I do *not* believe that prunes are an adequate substitute for butter in a cake. The result is often rubbery and unintentionally fruity. I like my prunes to stand up to my chocolate. So here's a prune-laced chocolate cake, bursting with flavor and a delicate texture, proud of its buttery heritage.

4 tablespoons (½ stick) unsalted butter
2 ounces unsweetened chocolate, broken
　　into pieces
¾ cup (6 ounces) lekvar (see Note)
1 cup sugar
Pinch of salt

1 tablespoon instant-coffee powder
¼ cup orange juice
1 tablespoon vanilla extract
2 eggs
½ teaspoon baking soda
1 cup flour

Preheat the oven to 350° F. Grease and flour an 8-inch layer pan.

In a large heavy saucepan over medium heat, begin melting the butter. When it's half melted, stir in the chocolate. Remove from the heat when the chocolate is half melted, and stir until the butter and chocolate are fully melted.

Add the lekvar, sugar, salt, coffee powder, orange juice, vanilla, and eggs. Add the baking soda in pinches, breaking up any lumps with your fingers. Stir in thoroughly. Stir in the flour, just until blended.

Pour and scrape the batter into the pan and bake for 45 minutes, or until a tester inserted in the center comes out clean. Cool in the pan on a rack for 10 minutes. Remove from the pan and cool on the rack for about 15 minutes more.

Makes 6 to 8 servings

NOTE: Lekvar, or prune butter, is available in gourmet shops and many super-markets.

Chocolate Pumpkin Spice Cake

This very moist, smooth cake combines the typical flavor of pumpkin pie with the sensual charms of chocolate. The chocolate flavor comes from Dutch-processed cocoa, a form of cocoa powder in which the acid in the chocolate has been neutralized with alkaline salts, creating a chocolate that's darker and richer in flavor than regular cocoa. It's the perfect balance for the rustic flavor of pumpkin and its inevitable spicy companions.

½ pound (2 sticks) unsalted butter
2 cups sugar
1 pound pumpkin puree, canned or
    homemade
1 tablespoon vanilla extract
4 eggs
2 teaspoons baking powder
1 teaspoon baking soda
¼ teaspoon salt

2 teaspoons ground cinnamon
1 teaspoon ground ginger
¼ teaspoon ground cloves
¼ teaspoon ground nutmeg
¾ cup Dutch-processed cocoa powder
2⅔ cups flour
1½ cups pecan or walnut pieces
1 cup golden raisins
1 cup confectioners' sugar (optional)

Preheat the oven to 350° F. Grease and flour a 10-inch bundt pan or tube pan.

In a large heavy saucepan over medium heat, melt the butter. Remove from the heat and mix in the sugar, pumpkin puree, vanilla, and eggs. Add the baking powder and baking soda in pinches, breaking up any lumps with your fingers. Stir in thoroughly. Stir in the salt, cinnamon, ginger, cloves, nutmeg, and cocoa. Stir in the flour, just until blended, then the nuts and raisins.

Pour and scrape the batter into the pan. Smooth the top. Bake for 45 minutes. Cool in the pan on a rack for 10 minutes. Remove from the pan and cool on the rack for about 15 minutes more. When cool, dust the top with confectioners' sugar, if desired.

Makes 14 to 16 servings

NOTE: Some Rummy Maple Icing (page 101) can be drizzled over the top of this cake instead of the sugar, although no icing is really needed.

COFFEE
CAKES

Traditional Sour Cream Coffee Cake

Easy Walnut Coffee Cake

Apple Coffee Cake

Chocolate Cinnamon Swirl Coffee Cake

Almond Orange Coffee Cake

Lemon Poppy Seed Cake

Black Pepper Gingerbread

Buttermilk Ginger Cake

Chocolate Chip Tea Cake

Vanilla Pine Nut Cake

In the glitzy world of pastry, coffee cakes remain puritanically plain. Shunning surface adornment, they keep their treasures close to the heart with coins of almond paste buried in a buttery cake or a necklace of dried fruit lying hidden in mounds of sour cream and cinnamon.

What makes coffee cakes extravagant is not their nature but the context in which they are served. They transform a simple cup of coffee into an elegant repast. And alongside scrambled eggs or cornmeal mush, even a plain coffee cake becomes the crown jewel of breakfast.

One-pot coffee cakes are similar to the other cakes in this book, but with one vital difference: In coffee cakes, the liquid is sour—whether yogurt, buttermilk, sour cream, citrus juice, molasses, or coffee. The unique chemistry of acid is what gives coffee cakes their delicate crumb and rich flavor.

Acids naturally soften the structure of a cake by breaking down the protein in the batter. Since it's the buildup of proteins that creates toughness, acidic liquids act as tenderizing agents. That's why buttermilk biscuits are so much lighter and more tender than other types of biscuits. And it's why a bit of yogurt in a cake batter will make the cake fluffier, or why sour cream makes a butter cake fine grained and soft without taking away any of its buttery richness.

Don't overdo it, though. Too much acid alters the balance between acid and base, which can interfere with the action of the baking powder in a recipe. Baking powder is balanced to give maximum rise with minimal leavener. But when an acid is part of the batter, the balance is thrown off. Baking soda is often used to bring the balance back in line, but baking soda has disadvantages too. Baking soda tends to release its leavening right away. So when a recipe uses only baking soda, it is important to get the cake into the oven as quickly as possible once the batter is mixed.

Several of the following cakes are baked in a bundt or tube pan. These doughnut-shaped pans help speed up the baking by circulating hot air more quickly around and through the cake. In addition, their ring shape is perfect for the softer structure of a coffee cake, which is often too delicate to maintain its structure across the eight- or nine-inch span of a layer pan or baking pan.

The difference between bundt and tube pans is slight. Bundt pans have rounded bottoms and a decorative pattern cast into the shape of the pan. Tube pans have flat, frequently removable, bottoms. Bundt cakes are always served upside down so that the rounded decorative side faces up. For most cakes, it makes no difference which you use. Usually, I prefer bundt pans because they bake a bit faster, but for cakes that have to face right side up, Apple Coffee Cake, for example, a tube pan is the only choice.

Traditional Sour Cream Coffee Cake

The streusel crumb topping that commonly graces the surface of a coffee cake is made by blending flour, butter, and sugar. It usually requires a separate bowl, a pastry cutter, and an extra recipe step. Here, the streusel is made instantly by crumbling shortbread cookies over the batter. The results are remarkably authentic, and why shouldn't they be? After all, what is shortbread but a blending of flour, butter, and sugar?

¼ pound (1 stick) unsalted butter

1 cup sugar

1 teaspoon vanilla extract

½ teaspoon ground cinnamon

Pinch of salt

1 cup sour cream, regular or lowfat

2 eggs

1½ teaspoons baking soda

1 teaspoon baking powder

2 cups flour

3 ounces shortbread cookies (12 Lorna Doone or 6 Pepperidge Farm cookies, for example)

Preheat the oven to 350° F. Grease an 8-inch layer pan.

In a large heavy saucepan over medium heat, melt the butter, stirring occasionally. Remove from the heat.

Stir in the sugar, vanilla, cinnamon, salt, sour cream, and eggs. Add the baking soda and baking powder in pinches, breaking up any lumps with your fingers. Stir thoroughly. Stir in the flour, just until well blended.

Pour and scrape the batter into the pan and crumble the shortbread cookies finely over the top. Bake for 40 to 45 minutes, or until a tester inserted in the center comes out clean. Cool on a rack for 10 minutes. Remove from the pan and cool on the rack for about 15 minutes more.

Makes 12 servings

Easy Walnut Coffee Cake

Let this recipe, a coffee cake loaded with walnuts, be your map for a world of rich sour-cream cakes inundated with nuts, candies, dried fruits, and crumbled cookies. As long as the additions are dry and kept to the same measurement, they will not interfere with how the cake rises or sets. This walnut coffee cake could become a recipe for Cherry Chocolate Chip Coffee Cake, Orange Hazelnut Coffee Cake, and on and on and on.

¼ pound (1 stick) unsalted butter
1½ cups sugar
1 cup sour cream, regular or lowfat
2 eggs
Pinch of salt
1 teaspoon ground cinnamon

1 teaspoon vanilla extract
1½ teaspoons baking soda
1 teaspoon baking powder
2 cups flour
2 cups walnut pieces

Preheat the oven to 350° F. Grease and flour a 9-inch square baking pan.

In a large heavy saucepan over medium heat, melt the butter, stirring occasionally. Remove from the heat.

Stir in the sugar, sour cream, eggs, salt, half the cinnamon, and the vanilla. Add the baking soda and baking powder in pinches, breaking up any lumps with your fingers. Stir in thoroughly. Stir in the flour, just until well blended, then 1½ cups of the walnuts.

Pour and scrape the batter into the pan and scatter the remaining walnuts and sprinkle the remaining cinnamon over the top of the cake. Bake for 45 to 50 minutes, or until a tester inserted in the center comes out clean. Cool in the pan on a rack for 10 minutes. Remove from the pan and cool on the rack for about 15 minutes more.

Makes 12 servings

Apple Coffee Cake

This cake is a real keeper. The apples continue to lend moisture to the cake during days of storage. If anything, the cake can get too wet if it is wrapped very tightly. Storing it on a plate under a tent of foil or a cake dome will preserve the cake's perfect consistency for up to five days.

½ pound (2 sticks) unsalted butter

2 cups sugar

2 teaspoons vanilla extract

1½ teaspoons ground cinnamon

Pinch of salt

1 cup sour cream, regular or lowfat

4 eggs

1 tablespoon baking soda

1 teaspoon baking powder

4 cups flour

1 can (20 ounces) sliced apples, drained

Preheat the oven to 350° F. Grease and flour a 10-inch tube pan.

In a large heavy saucepan over medium heat, melt the butter, stirring occasionally. Remove from the heat.

Stir in the sugar, vanilla, 1 teaspoon of the cinnamon, salt, sour cream, and eggs. Add the baking soda and baking powder in pinches, breaking up any lumps with your fingers. Stir thoroughly. Stir in the flour, just until well blended.

Spread half the batter in the pan in an even layer. Top with half the apples, then with the rest of the batter. Spread the top level and arrange the rest of the apples evenly over the top of the cake. Sprinkle with the remaining cinnamon. Bake for 55 to 60 minutes, or until a tester inserted in one of the cracks in the top of the cake comes out almost clean. Cool on a rack for 15 minutes. Remove from the pan and cool on the rack for about 10 minutes more.

Makes 12 servings

Chocolate Cinnamon Swirl Coffee Cake

This combination of chocolate, nuts, fruit, and cinnamon is reminiscent of rich Slavic pastries. All the ingredients should be well distributed and of similar size. Instead of using chopped chocolate, I use plain chocolate cookies that can be crumbled and dispersed through the cake without any chopping.

½ pound (2 sticks) unsalted butter

2 cups sugar

2 teaspoons vanilla extract

¼ teaspoon salt

2 cups sour cream, regular or lowfat

3 eggs

1½ teaspoons baking soda

1½ teaspoons baking powder

3 cups flour

½ cup crumbled chocolate wafers
  (6 to 8, depending on size)

½ cup walnut pieces

¼ cup dried currants or chopped raisins

1 tablespoon ground cinnamon

Preheat the oven to 350° F. Grease and flour a 10-inch bundt pan.

In a large heavy saucepan over medium heat, melt the butter, stirring occasionally. Remove from the heat.

Stir in the sugar, vanilla, salt, sour cream, and eggs. Add the baking soda and baking powder in pinches, breaking up any lumps with your fingers. Stir in thoroughly. Stir in the flour, just until well blended. Mound the crumbled chocolate wafers, walnuts, currants, and cinnamon on top of the batter. Swirl them into the batter, stirring no more than 5 times.

Pour and scrape the batter into the pan and bake for 50 to 55 minutes, or until a tester inserted in the center comes out clean. Cool in the pan on a rack for 10 minutes. Invert, remove the pan, and cool on the rack for about 15 minutes more.

Makes 12 servings

Almond Orange Coffee Cake

This cake, very fine grained and buttery, gets its almond flavor from three sources. Almond pastry filling is blended with butter to form the structural base for the batter. This is flavored with almond liqueur. Then, finely ground almonds replace a third of the flour. The effect is almond through and through without the overpowering addition of almond extract that mars the natural flavor of so many almond cakes.

½ pound (2 sticks) unsalted butter

1 can (12½ ounces) almond filling

2 tablespoons dried orange peel

1 cup sugar

Pinch of salt

2 teaspoons vanilla extract

¼ cup amaretto

4 eggs

1 tablespoon baking powder

2 cups flour

1 cup ground almonds

Preheat the oven to 350° F. Grease and flour a 10-inch bundt pan.

In a large heavy saucepan over medium heat, melt the butter, stirring occasionally. Remove from the heat.

Stir in the almond filling, orange peel, sugar, salt, vanilla, amaretto, and eggs. Add the baking powder in pinches, breaking up any lumps with your fingers. Stir in thoroughly. Stir in the flour and ground almonds, just until well blended.

Pour and scrape the batter into the pan and bake for 45 minutes, or until a tester inserted in the center comes out clean. Cool in the pan on a rack for 10 minutes. Invert, remove the pan, and cool on the rack for about 15 minutes more.

Makes 12 servings

Lemon Poppy Seed Cake

Many people react with surprise at the notion of poppy seeds in a cake. I grew up on the stuff and have always loved it. This buttery cake has the perfume of lemon, the delicate tang of sour cream, and the crunch of lots of tiny poppy seeds. Poppy seed filling is sold in most supermarkets alongside canned and jarred pie fillings.

½ pound (2 sticks) unsalted butter

1 can (12½ ounces) poppy seed filling

1 tablespoon dried lemon peel

1 cup sugar

Pinch of salt

1 cup sour cream, regular or lowfat

4 eggs

1 tablespoon vanilla extract

2 teaspoons baking soda

2½ cups flour

Preheat the oven to 350° F. Grease and flour a 10-inch bundt pan.

In a large heavy saucepan over medium heat, melt the butter, stirring occasionally. Remove from the heat.

Stir in the poppy seed filling, lemon peel, sugar, salt, sour cream, eggs, and vanilla. Add the baking soda in pinches, breaking up any lumps with your fingers. Stir thoroughly. Stir in the flour, just until well blended.

Pour and scrape the batter into the pan and bake for 45 minutes, or until a tester inserted in the center comes out clean. Cool in the pan on a rack for 10 minutes. Invert, remove the pan, and cool on the rack for about 15 minutes more.

Makes 12 servings

Black Pepper Gingerbread

If you love gingerbread, this one's for you. The traditional ginger-cinnamon-nutmeg triumvirate is revolutionized in an unexpected way—with a jolt of mustard and black pepper. The mustard and pepper underscore the ginger and lend heat and aroma for a flavor that's intense but not shocking. A scoop of ice cream provides a cooling counterpoint.

¼ pound (1 stick) unsalted butter
½ cup (packed) dark brown sugar
1 cup dark molasses
1 teaspoon spicy brown mustard
2 tablespoons instant-coffee powder
2 eggs
1 tablespoon ground ginger

1 teaspoon ground cinnamon
½ teaspoon ground allspice
1 teaspoon ground black pepper
Pinch of salt
2 teaspoons baking soda
2⅓ cups flour
1 cup very hot water

Preheat the oven to 375° F. Grease a 9-inch square baking pan.

In a heavy saucepan over medium heat, melt the butter. Remove from the heat.

Mix in the brown sugar, molasses, mustard, coffee, and eggs, stirring until smooth. Add the ginger, cinnamon, allspice, black pepper, and salt. Add the baking soda in pinches, breaking up any lumps with your fingers. Stir until well blended. Mix in the flour, stirring just until blended. Stir in the water.

Pour and scrape the batter into the pan and bake for 40 to 45 minutes, or until the cake is springy and a tester inserted in the center comes out with just a few crumbs clinging to it. Cool in the pan on a rack for 10 minutes. Remove from the pan and cool on the rack for about 15 minutes more. Serve warm or cooled.

Makes 9 to 12 servings

Buttermilk Ginger Cake

This ginger cake is lighter and more delicate than the Black Pepper Gingerbread. Its flavor comes from two different forms of ginger—dried and fresh—for three different effects. The dried ginger is for heat, the fresh for aroma, the combination for a burst of flavor that grows with every bite.

12 tablespoons (1½ sticks) unsalted butter
1¼ cups (packed) dark brown sugar
1 cup granulated sugar
2 teaspoons vanilla extract
½ teaspoon salt
3 eggs
1½ teaspoons ground ginger

2 teaspoons grated fresh gingerroot
1½ teaspoons baking soda
1½ cups buttermilk
2 cups all-purpose flour
1 cup whole-wheat flour or 1 more cup
    all-purpose flour

Preheat the oven to 350° F. Grease and flour a 10-inch tube pan.

In a large heavy saucepan over medium heat, melt the butter, stirring occasionally. Remove from the heat.

Stir in the brown sugar, granulated sugar, vanilla, salt, eggs, ground ginger, and fresh ginger. Add the baking soda in pinches, breaking up any lumps with your fingers. Stir in thoroughly. Stir in the buttermilk. Stir in the flour, just until well blended.

Pour and scrape the batter into the pan and bake for 1 hour to 1 hour 5 minutes, or until a tester inserted in the center comes out clean. Cool in the pan on a rack for 10 minutes. Remove from the pan and cool on the rack for about 15 minutes more.

Makes 12 servings

Chocolate Chip Tea Cake

This coffee cake is freckled with tiny chocolate chips. Because the chips are small, they are apt to melt if the batter is too hot when they are added. So make sure the butter is removed from the heat when it's no more than halfway melted and that the sour cream is cold. The resulting loaf is very tender, rich, and delicate.

6 tablespoons (¾ stick) unsalted butter

¾ cup sugar

1 teaspoon vanilla extract

¼ teaspoon salt

1 cup cold sour cream, regular or lowfat

1 egg

¾ teaspoon baking soda

¾ teaspoon baking powder

1½ cups flour

¾ cup mini chocolate chips

Preheat the oven to 350° F. Grease and flour a 9-inch loaf pan.

In a large heavy saucepan over medium heat, begin melting the butter, stirring occasionally. When it's half melted, remove the pan from the heat and stir until fully melted.

Stir in the sugar, vanilla, salt, sour cream, and egg. Add the baking soda and baking powder in pinches, breaking up any lumps with your fingers. Stir thoroughly. Stir in the flour, just until blended, then the chocolate chips.

Pour and scrape the batter into the pan and bake for 45 to 50 minutes, or until a tester inserted in the middle comes out with just a crumb clinging to it. Cool on a rack for 10 minutes. Remove from the pan and cool on the rack for about 15 minutes more.

Makes 12 servings

Vanilla Pine Nut Cake

Of all the commonly available nuts, pine nuts are the only ones that have not entered into our national baking repertoire. We grind them into pesto and toss them on a sautéed fish, but mix them into cake? Never. Here's a reason to change. This buttery cake is infused with the subtle flavor of pine nuts toasted as the cake bakes.

¼ pound (1 stick) unsalted butter

1 cup granulated sugar

1 cup lowfat or nonfat vanilla yogurt

2 teaspoons vanilla extract

⅛ teaspoon salt

2 eggs

1½ teaspoons baking soda

1 teaspoon baking powder

2 cups flour

⅓ cup pine nuts, coarsely chopped

2 tablespoons dark brown sugar

Preheat the oven to 350° F. Grease an 8-inch layer pan.

In a large heavy saucepan over medium heat, melt the butter, stirring occasionally. Remove from the heat.

Stir in the granulated sugar, yogurt, vanilla, salt, and eggs. Add the baking soda and baking powder in pinches, breaking up any lumps with your fingers. Stir thoroughly. Stir in the flour, just until well blended.

Pour and scrape the batter into the pan and scatter the pine nuts over the top, pressing gently into the surface. Sprinkle with the brown sugar. Bake for 40 to 45 minutes, or until a tester inserted in the center comes out clean. Cool on a rack for 10 minutes. Remove the pan and cool on the rack for about 15 minutes more.

Makes 12 servings

CUP CAKES

Chocolate Chip Raspberry-filled Cupcakes

Orange Buttermilk Cupcakes

Vanilla Butter Cupcakes

Chocolate Birthday Cupcakes

Bleeding-Heart Chocolate Cupcakes

Whole Wheat–Butterscotch Cupcakes

Banana–White Chocolate–Cherry Cupcakes

Honey Cupcakes

Spiced Fruited Cupcakes

Crumb Cupcakes

A cupcake is just for you. Unlike large cakes, which call for a crowd, a cupcake wants only a single mouth to please. And how it does that is as individual as any relationship can be between an eater and a sweet, whether you eat it icing first, from the bottom up, or sliced like a miniature birthday cake.

Fortunately, the extravagance of cupcakes is all in the eating. From batter to baking, they are quicker than cookies and easier than pie. Following the one-pot method, none of these cupcakes takes more than ten minutes to mix up or more than twenty minutes to bake.

All of them bake in a standard nonstick 12-cup tin, where each cupcake cup has a capacity of ½ cup and a top diameter of 3 inches. Because cupcakes are notorious stickers, I always use a nonstick muffin tin and spray a thin film of vegetable oil inside the cups. If your tin doesn't have a nonstick coating, consider using lining papers. Either way will spare you from greasing and flouring the inside of each cup, an easy but messy chore.

Fill each cup no more than three-quarters of the way. The only exception is for a dense-battered or very chunky recipe, such as the Banana–White Chocolate–Cherry or Spiced Fruited Cupcakes. These cakes tend to rise only minimally, so mounding the batter almost up to the rim will get an impressive looking result. But do not fill the cup completely or the cake will expand over the top and form a cap, making the finished cupcake look more like a muffin.

It's usually not necessary to test the doneness of cupcakes with a skewer or pick. Check on the baking about five minutes before you think they might be done. If they are wet on top, give them another five minutes and check again. If they are dry, press in the center; a finished cupcake will spring back but will still feel soft. Do not wait for cupcakes to pull away from the sides of the tin, as you would when testing layer or sheet cake. By the time that happens, the cupcake will be overcooked.

When checking for doneness, look at cupcakes in different parts of the pan. Those near the edge tend to bake faster than those in the center. If they are baking unevenly, turn the pan once during baking.

Chocolate Chip Raspberry-filled Cupcakes

Fluffy with sour cream and loaded with chocolate chips, these extra-large cupcakes don't stop with a rich batter. They are topped with a dollop of raspberry filling that descends into the heart of the cupcake as it bakes, ready to seep into each bite.

6 tablespoons (¾ stick) unsalted butter

¾ cup sugar

1 teaspoon vanilla extract

1 teaspoon lemon juice

Pinch of salt

1 cup sour cream

1 egg

¾ teaspoon baking soda

¾ teaspoon baking powder

1½ cups flour

½ cup mini chocolate chips

6 tablespoons raspberry filling or seedless raspberry jam

Preheat the oven to 350° F. Grease or line a 12-cup standard muffin tin.

In a large heavy saucepan over medium heat, melt the butter, stirring occasionally. Remove from the heat.

Stir in the sugar, vanilla, lemon juice, salt, sour cream, and egg. Add the baking soda and baking powder in pinches, breaking up any lumps with your fingers. Stir thoroughly. Stir in the flour, just until well blended. Stir in the chocolate chips.

Spoon the batter into the muffin tin, filling each cup about three-quarters full. Place ½ tablespoon of the raspberry filling on top of each cupcake. Bake for 20 minutes, or until cupcakes are springy and fully puffed. Cool on a rack for 5 minutes. Remove the cupcakes from the pan and cool on the rack for at least 10 minutes more.

Makes 12 servings

Orange Buttermilk Cupcakes

The secret of these delicate silken cupcakes is one of the magic charms of baking—buttermilk. Buttermilk softens the fiber of cakes and underscores all the other flavors in a batter, particularly fruit flavors. In this recipe, the results are dramatic. Orange extract ensures full flavor throughout the cake, while bits of dried orange peel release their perfume with every bite.

6 tablespoons (¾ stick) unsalted butter	Pinch of salt
1 cup sugar	2 eggs
1 teaspoon vanilla extract	¾ teaspoon baking soda
½ teaspoon orange extract	¾ cup buttermilk
1 tablespoon dried orange peel	1½ cups flour

Preheat the oven to 350° F. Grease or line a 12-cup standard muffin tin.

In a large heavy saucepan over medium heat, melt the butter, stirring occasionally. Remove from the heat.

Stir in the sugar, vanilla, orange extract, orange peel, salt, and eggs. Add the baking soda in pinches, breaking up any lumps with your fingers. Stir thoroughly. Stir in the buttermilk and the flour, just until well blended.

Spoon the batter into the muffin tin, filling each cup about three-quarters full. Bake for 15 minutes, or until cupcakes are springy and fully puffed. Cool on a rack for 5 minutes. Lift out the cupcakes and cool on the rack for at least 10 minutes more.

Makes 12 servings

NOTE: Not that they need any adornment, but some Chocolate Sour Cream Icing (page 97) or Chocolate Cream Cheese Icing (page 98) wouldn't hurt these cakes.

Vanilla Butter Cupcakes

These rich, buttery cakes are sublimely plain. Extra butter ensures their tender texture as does the use of cornstarch for a portion of the flour. The combination of cornstarch and all-purpose flour mimics the softening effect that cake flour has on a batter yet lets you avoid storing an extra type of flour in your cupboard.

½ pound (2 sticks) unsalted butter

1 cup sugar

2 teaspoons vanilla extract

Pinch of salt

3 eggs

1 teaspoon baking powder

1 cup flour

¼ cup cornstarch

1 tablespoon dried lemon peel (optional)

Preheat the oven to 350° F. Grease or line a 12-cup standard muffin tin.

In a large heavy saucepan over medium heat, melt the butter, stirring occasionally. Remove from the heat.

Stir in the sugar, vanilla, salt, and eggs. Add the baking powder in pinches, breaking up any lumps with your fingers. Stir thoroughly. Stir in the flour, just until well blended. Stir in the cornstarch until the batter is smooth. Stir in the lemon peel, if desired.

Spoon the batter into the muffin tin, filling each cup about three-quarters full. Bake for 15 to 20 minutes, or until cupcakes are springy and fully puffed. Cool on a rack for 5 minutes. Lift out the cupcakes and cool on the rack for at least 10 minutes more.

Makes 12 servings

NOTE: For a birthday party, these cakes could be topped with Chocolate Sour Cream Icing (page 97), Lemon Icing (page 102), or White Chocolate–Cream Cheese Icing (page 99).

Chocolate Birthday Cupcakes

Brown sugar adds depth and richness to chocolate cakes. Much of the flavor of chocolate comes from how the cocoa beans are roasted. The same caramel quality that develops during roasting is present in the molasses of brown sugar, reinforcing the chocolate.

6 tablespoons (¾ stick) unsalted butter

2 ounces unsweetened chocolate, broken into pieces

1¼ cups (packed) dark brown sugar

1 teaspoon vanilla extract

Pinch of salt

2 eggs

1 teaspoon baking soda

1¼ cups flour

½ cup very hot water

Preheat the oven to 350° F. Grease or line a 12-cup standard muffin tin.

In a large heavy saucepan over medium heat, begin melting the butter. When it's half melted, stir in the chocolate and continue cooking, stirring constantly, until the chocolate is half melted. Remove from the heat and stir until the butter and chocolate are completely melted.

Stir in the brown sugar, vanilla, salt, and eggs. Add the baking soda in pinches, breaking up any lumps with your fingers. Stir thoroughly. Stir in the flour, just until well blended. Stir in the hot water.

Spoon the batter into the muffin tin, filling each cup about three-quarters full. Bake for 15 to 20 minutes, or until cupcakes are springy and fully puffed. Cool on a rack for 5 minutes. Lift out the cupcakes and cool on the rack for at least 10 minutes.

Makes 12 servings

NOTE: Top these cupcakes with Chocolate Sour Cream Icing (page 97), White Chocolate–Cream Cheese Icing (page 99), or Chocolate Mint Icing (page 99).

Bleeding-Heart Chocolate Cupcakes

If there were an X-rating for desserts, these luscious little cakes would be tagged "adults only." Not too sweet and loaded with chocolate, the cupcakes will appear sunken and underdone when they emerge from the oven, but don't let their ugly-duckling appearance fool you. The flavor is overwhelming and their moussy middles ooze with every bite.

½ pound (2 sticks) unsalted butter
8 ounces semisweet chocolate, broken
   into pieces
¾ cup sugar

½ teaspoon vanilla extract
7 eggs
Pinch of salt
7 tablespoons flour

Preheat the oven to 325° F. Grease and flour a 12-cup standard muffin tin.

In a large heavy saucepan over medium heat, begin melting the butter, stirring occasionally. When it's half melted, add the chocolate and continue cooking until the chocolate is half melted. Remove from the heat and continue stirring until mixture is smooth.

Mix in the sugar, vanilla, eggs, and salt until smooth. Mix in the flour, just until blended.

Ladle the batter into the muffin tin, filling each cup about three-quarters full. Bake for 15 minutes until the edges are set but the centers are still very wet and sunken. Cool on a rack for 5 minutes. Run a knife around the edge of each cupcake and carefully remove to a cooling rack. Cool for 10 minutes more. Serve warm.

Makes 12 servings

Whole Wheat–Butterscotch Cupcakes

I am not a big proponent of fortifying sweets with whole-grain flour. Too often, the results are leaden without delivering enough health benefit to make the sacrifice worthwhile. These cupcakes are an exception to that rule. The nutty flavor of whole wheat flour is just right with the rich caramel flavors of molasses and toffee chips.

6 tablespoons (¾ stick) unsalted butter

⅔ cup sugar

⅓ cup dark molasses

1 teaspoon vanilla extract

Pinch of salt

2 eggs

¾ teaspoon baking soda

⅔ cup buttermilk

¾ cup all-purpose flour

¾ cup whole wheat flour

¾ cup toffee chips

Preheat the oven to 350° F. Grease or line a 12-cup standard muffin tin.

In a large heavy saucepan over medium heat, melt the butter, stirring occasionally. Remove from the heat.

Stir in the sugar, molasses, vanilla, salt, and eggs. Add the baking soda in pinches, breaking up any lumps with your fingers. Stir thoroughly. Stir in the buttermilk and the all-purpose and whole wheat flours, just until well blended. Stir in the toffee chips.

Spoon the batter into the muffin tin, filling each cup about three-quarters full. Bake for 15 minutes, or until cupcakes are springy and fully puffed. Cool on a rack for 5 minutes. Lift out the cupcakes and cool on the rack for at least 10 minutes more.

Makes 12 servings

NOTE: If you must ice, top these cupcakes with Rummy Maple Icing (page 101), Chestnut Buttercream (page 102), or Coffee Icing (page 98).

Banana–White Chocolate–Cherry Cupcakes

These cupcakes are wild, full of creamy bananas, chewy cherries, and lots of chocolate. The batter is mixed with a fork so you can mash the bananas while blending in the other ingredients. Because chunks of cherries and chocolate will be added to the batter, you needn't concern yourself with mashing the bananas until they're smooth. A few banana bits will only increase the textural interest of these cupcakes.

¼ pound (1 stick) unsalted butter
1 cup sugar
1 teaspoon vanilla extract
3 ripe bananas
¼ cup sour cream
2 eggs

1 teaspoon baking soda
½ teaspoon baking powder
2 cups flour
⅓ cup dried cherries, chopped
⅓ cup white chocolate chips

Preheat the oven to 350° F. Grease or line a 12-cup standard muffin tin.

In a large heavy saucepan over medium heat, melt the butter. Remove from the heat.

Add the sugar, vanilla, and bananas and mix together, mashing the bananas with the back of a fork until mostly incorporated. Stir in the sour cream and eggs. Add the baking soda and baking powder in pinches, breaking up any lumps with your fingers. Stir in thoroughly. Stir in the flour, just until blended. Stir in the cherries and the chips.

Spoon the batter into the muffin tin, filling each cup almost full. Bake for 15 to 18 minutes, or until the cupcakes are springy and fully puffed. Cool on a rack for 5 minutes. Lift out the cupcakes and cool on the rack for at least 10 minutes more.

Makes 12 servings

NOTE: If you're feeling especially decadent, top these with White Chocolate–Cream Cheese Icing (page 99).

Honey Cupcakes

Honey is laced with orange, cinnamon, brown sugar, and coffee to create a wondrous combination of flavors and scents. Unlike other honey cakes that bowl you over with honey, these are both more subtle and more intense.

3 tablespoons unsalted butter
½ cup (packed) dark brown sugar
½ cup honey
2 teaspoons dried orange peel
½ teaspoon ground cinnamon
Pinch of salt

2 eggs
½ teaspoon baking soda
½ teaspoon baking powder
1½ cups flour
½ cup cold coffee, apple juice,
    or prune juice

Preheat the oven to 350° F. Grease or line a 12-cup standard muffin tin.

In a large heavy saucepan over medium heat, melt the butter, stirring occasionally. Remove from the heat.

Stir in the brown sugar, honey, orange peel, cinnamon, salt, and eggs. Add the baking soda and baking powder in pinches, breaking up any lumps with your fingers. Stir thoroughly. Stir in the flour, just until well blended. Stir in the coffee or juice.

Ladle the batter into the muffin tin, filling each cup about three-quarters full.

Bake for 15 to 18 minutes, or until cupcakes are springy and fully puffed. Cool on a rack for 5 minutes. Lift out the cupcakes and cool on the rack for at least 10 minutes more.

Makes 12 servings

NOTE: These cupcakes could be dressed up with Lemon Icing (page 102), Chestnut Buttercream (page 102), or Brandy Cream Cheese Icing (page 97).

Spiced Fruited Cupcakes

Even if you hate, abhor, and loathe fruitcake, you will love these cupcakes. Chockful of dried fruit (none of that nasty candied fruit here), spices, and nuts, they are fragrant and filling. When dividing the batter among the cupcake cups, make sure that the fruit and nuts are distributed evenly.

4 tablespoons (½ stick) unsalted butter
¼ cup (packed) dark brown sugar
½ cup dark corn syrup
1 tablespoon instant-coffee powder
1 tablespoon dried orange peel
2 teaspoons ground ginger
1 teaspoon ground cinnamon
¼ teaspoon ground cloves

Pinch of salt
1 egg
1 teaspoon baking soda
1 cup plus 2 tablespoons flour
½ cup hot water
2 cups mixed dried fruit pieces
1 cup walnut or pecan pieces

Preheat the oven to 350° F. Grease or line a 12-cup standard muffin tin.

In a large heavy saucepan over medium heat, melt the butter, stirring occasionally. Remove from the heat.

Stir in the brown sugar, corn syrup, coffee powder, orange peel, ginger, cinnamon, clove, salt, and egg. Add the baking soda in pinches, breaking up any lumps with your fingers. Stir thoroughly. Stir in the flour, just until well blended. Stir in the water, then the dried fruit and nuts.

Spoon the batter into the muffin tin, filling each cup almost to the top. Bake for 20 minutes, or until the cupcakes are springy and fully puffed. Cool on a rack for 5 minutes. Lift out the cupcakes and cool for at least 10 minutes more.

Makes 12 servings

Crumb Cupcakes

These coffee-cake cupcakes use the same topping trick as the Traditional Sour Cream Coffee Cake on page 20—crumbling shortbread cookies. Unlike most cupcakes, these are better suited to breakfast, brunch, or a coffee break, than to dessert.

¼ pound (1 stick) unsalted butter
1 cup sugar
1 teaspoon vanilla extract
½ teaspoon ground cinnamon
Pinch of salt
1 cup sour cream
2 eggs

1½ teaspoons baking soda
1 teaspoon baking powder
2 cups flour
3 ounces shortbread cookies (12 Lorna
    Doone or 6 Pepperidge Farm cookies,
    for example)

Preheat oven to 350° F. Grease or line a 12-cup standard muffin tin and set aside.

In a large heavy saucepan over medium heat, melt the butter, stirring occasionally. Remove from the heat.

Stir in the sugar, vanilla, cinnamon, salt, sour cream, and eggs. Add the baking soda and baking powder in pinches, breaking up any lumps with your fingers. Stir thoroughly. Stir in the flour, just until well blended.

Spoon the batter into the muffin tin, filling each cup about three-quarters full. Finely crumble the shortbread cookies over the cupcakes. Bake for 20 minutes, or until cupcakes are springy and fully puffed. Cool on a rack for 5 minutes. Remove the cupcakes from the pan and cool on the rack for at least 10 minutes more.

Makes 12 servings

FLOURLESS
CAKES

Chocolate Almond Torte

Black Coffee Torte

S'mores Torte

Cassis Torte

Triple Chocolate Bypass

Almost-A-Linzer Torte

Toasted Coconut Torte

Perfectly Plain Cheesecake

Cognac Pumpkin Cheesecake

Cannoli Cheese Torte

❖

The fastest way to determine exactly what a specific ingredient in a rec-ipe does is to leave it out. Try making a fat-free cake and the necessity of butter or oil becomes instantly clear. Omit the sugar and you'll likely end up with something closer to a dog biscuit than a *biscuit de noix*. But remove the flour and you'll discover the moistest, richest, lushest cake-confections that are apt to come out of an oven.

Some of the most prestigious cakes shun flour. In nut tortes, meringue dacquoises, cheesecakes, and mousse cakes, flour is replaced with other starchy ingredients—or none at all.

Flour surrogates can be graham cracker and cookie crumbs, bread crumbs, shredded coconut, cornstarch, or, the most common of all, ground nuts. Just about any nut will do, but in keeping with the principles of this book, the recipes in this chapter have been written only for nuts that are sold already ground.

Flour gives a cake flexibility and strength, and no other ingredient can duplicate those qualities. That's why flourless cakes are more likely to break when they are removed from the pan. It helps to line the bottom of the baking pan with wax paper so that if the cake sticks, it will stick to the paper rather than the bottom of the pan.

The cake will then slip from the pan along with the paper, which can then be peeled off easily.

Some flourless cakes use no flour substitute at all. Usually, these cakes have enough egg or rich ingredient in their formula to make the structural role of flour unnecessary. Such is the case with cheesecakes and rich dense chocolate mousse cakes.

I've been fiddling with cheesecake recipes for more than twenty-five years and through much trial and error came up with a technique that yields a flawless cake—without a blemish or crack on its surface and with a heart as smooth as custard. The secret is not in the ingredients (any cheesecake can reach this state of perfection), but in the baking. Slow it down. And when I say slow, I mean it. Set the oven at 200° F. and bake the cake for eight hours. At that temperature, the ingredients just meld and the cake emerges pristine, without a trace of graininess.

The baking time is trimmed in the cheesecake recipes in this chapter. Although the surface is a bit more blemished, the interior is almost as silken as the eight-hour, gold standard version. If you can plan your baking a day ahead, though, you'll get even better results. The easiest way is to start baking just before you go to bed and take out the finished dessert in the morning. Finally, a cake that literally bakes while you sleep.

Chocolate Almond Torte

This is a classic French chocolate cake, dense and moist, swoonably chocolate. Suitable for the most elegant occasions, its ease belies its sophistication. Because it contains no leavener, this cake doesn't rise or fall. Rather, its ingredients meld into a moist chocolate mass, embellished with a faint crunch of crushed nuts.

¼ pound (1 stick) unsalted butter

4 ounces semisweet chocolate, broken into pieces

⅔ cup sugar

3 eggs

1⅔ cups ground almonds (8 ounces)

1 teaspoon vanilla extract

¼ teaspoon almond extract

Preheat the oven to 375° F. Spray the bottom and sides of an 8-inch layer pan with spray shortening, line the bottom of the pan with wax paper or foil, spray with more shortening, and dust with flour.

In a large heavy saucepan over medium heat, begin melting the butter. When it's half melted, add the chocolate and stir until the chocolate is half melted. Remove from heat and stir until both are fully melted.

Mix in the sugar. Mix in the eggs, ground almonds, vanilla, and almond extract.

Pour and scrape the batter into the pan and bake for 25 minutes, or until a tester inserted in the center of the cake comes out with a damp crumb clinging to it. Cool in the pan on a rack for 20 minutes. Run a knife around the edge of the cake, cover with wax paper, and invert onto a plate. Remove the pan and peel off lining paper. Cover with a rack and invert. Remove the plate and wax paper and cool about 15 minutes more.

Makes 10 servings

NOTE: This cake can be finished with French Chocolate Glaze (page 100) or simply dusted with confectioners' sugar. To make a decorative pattern, place a lacy doily over the cake, and sift the powdered sugar over the doily. When you lift the doily, its pattern will be stenciled over the top of the cake.

Black Coffee Torte

This cake is damp, rich, and overcome with dark roasted coffee flavor. No icing is needed, but a piping of whipped cream probably would not go unappreciated.

12 tablespoons (1½ sticks) unsalted butter
1⅔ cups ground walnuts (8 ounces)
2 tablespoons instant-coffee powder
1 cup sugar
3 eggs

¼ cup dry bread crumbs
Pinch of salt
1 teaspoon vanilla extract
2 tablespoons coffee-flavored liqueur or
　　rum or brandy

Preheat the oven to 375° F. Spray the bottom and sides of an 8-inch layer pan with spray shortening, line the bottom of the pan with parchment or wax paper, spray with more shortening, and dust with flour.

In a large heavy saucepan over medium heat, begin melting the butter. After about 30 seconds, add the ground walnuts and stir until the butter is completely melted and the walnuts are lightly toasted. Remove from the heat. Mix in the coffee powder and sugar until well blended. Mix in the eggs, bread crumbs, salt, vanilla, and liqueur.

Pour the batter into the pan and bake for 25 minutes, or until a tester inserted in the center of the cake comes out with a damp crumb clinging to it. Cool in the pan on a rack for 20 minutes. Run a knife around the edge of the cake, cover with wax paper, and invert onto a plate. Remove the pan and peel off the lining paper. Cover with a rack and invert. Remove the plate and wax paper and cool about 15 minutes more.

Makes 10 servings

S'mores Torte

The inspired ménage à trois of milk chocolate, graham crackers, and marshmallows is for most of us our first food-borne intoxication. I, for one, have never outgrown its allure. Unlike a campfire s'more, which maintains a textural distinction between the crunch of the cracker, the ooze of chocolate, and the sticky smear of marshmallow, this cake combines all those elements for a truly gooey extravagance.

¼ pound (1 stick) unsalted butter

3 Hershey milk chocolate bars (1.55 ounces each), broken into pieces

⅔ cup sugar

3 eggs

1 teaspoon vanilla extract

2 cups graham cracker crumbs

1½ cups mini marshmallows

Preheat the oven to 350° F. Spray the bottom and sides of an 8-inch layer pan with spray shortening, line the bottom of the pan with parchment or wax paper, spray with more shortening, and dust with flour or graham cracker crumbs.

In a large heavy saucepan over medium heat, begin melting the butter. When it's half melted, add the chocolate and stir until chocolate is half melted. Remove from heat and stir until both are fully melted.

Mix in the sugar, eggs, vanilla, graham cracker crumbs, and marshmallows.

Pour and scrape the batter into the pan and bake for 30 minutes, or until the top is browned, the edges are crusty, and only the very center is still soft. Cool in the pan on a rack for 20 minutes. Run a knife around the edge of the cake, cover with wax paper, and invert onto a plate. Remove the pan and peel off the lining paper. Cover with a rack and invert. Remove plate and wax paper and cool about 15 minutes more.

Makes 10 servings

Cassis Torte

Cassis, the black-currant liqueur of northern Burgundy, is as wonderful in baking as it is in a classic kir. Unlike other fruit liquors, which tend to fade to the background in a cake or torte, the perfume of cassis seems to blossom in the warmth of the oven. In this recipe, it is further enhanced by a healthy outpouring of dried red currants. This recipe starts differently from the others in this book—by simmering the dried fruit in water for a few minutes in order to soften it.

1 cup dried currants
¼ cup water
¼ pound (1 stick) unsalted butter
2 ounces white chocolate,
   broken into pieces
½ cup sugar

3 eggs
¼ cup crème de cassis
1 tablespoon dried orange peel
⅔ cup dry bread crumbs
1 teaspoon vanilla extract
½ teaspoon baking powder

Preheat the oven to 350° F. Grease the bottom and sides of an 8-inch layer pan, line the bottom of the pan with parchment or wax paper, grease the paper, and dust with flour or bread crumbs.

In a large heavy saucepan, combine the currants and water. Cook over medium heat until all the water has been absorbed, about 2 minutes. Add the butter and begin melting it. When it's half melted, add the chocolate, and stir until the chocolate is half melted. Remove from heat and stir until the butter and chocolate are fully melted.

Mix in the sugar. Mix in the eggs, cassis, orange peel, bread crumbs, and vanilla. Add the baking powder in pinches to break up any lumps and mix in thoroughly.

Pour and scrape the batter into the pan and bake for 25 minutes, or until a tester inserted in the center of the cake comes out with a damp crumb clinging to it. Cool in the pan on a rack for 20 minutes. Run a knife around the edge of the cake, cover with wax paper, and invert onto a plate. Remove the pan and peel off the lining paper. Cover with a rack and invert. Remove the plate and wax paper and cool about 15 minutes more.

Makes 10 servings

Triple Chocolate Bypass

If the notion of too much chocolate is meaningless to you, this recipe should stand as a reality check. The cake mixes up in seconds and bakes in twenty-three minutes. Don't over-bake it. When you take it out of the oven, it will look like a chocolate pond. That's fine. Let it cool and then refrigerate it for several hours until it is firm. Serve in thin slices, preferably with some berries or slices of citrus to help restore consciousness between bites.

1 cup milk

1 tablespoon instant-coffee powder

1 pound semisweet chocolate, broken into pieces

1 tablespoon vanilla extract

2 tablespoons orange liqueur

½ pound (2 sticks) unsalted butter

5 eggs

Preheat the oven to 350° F. Grease the sides and bottom of a 9-inch springform pan, and line the bottom with parchment or wax paper. Grease the paper.

In a large heavy saucepan, heat the milk until simmering. Turn the heat to low, add the coffee powder and chocolate, and stir until the chocolate has melted. Remove from the heat.

Add the vanilla, liqueur, and butter and stir until smooth. Mix in the eggs.

Pour the batter into the pan, and bake for 23 minutes. The cake will look undone. Remove it from the oven, let cool, and refrigerate until firm. Run a knife around the sides and remove the springform.

Makes 16 servings

Almost-A-Linzer Torte

This rendition converts the traditional spiced pastry into an easy-to-handle crumb mixture, half of which is pressed into a pan and covered with raspberry jam. The rest of the crumbs are scattered on top. The torte bakes up into a crunchy, nut-filled fruit bar.

¼ pound (1 stick) unsalted butter
½ cup (packed) dark brown sugar
1 teaspoon ground cinnamon
Pinch ground cloves
1 tablespoon dried lemon peel

Pinch of salt
1 cup cornstarch
About 1 cup ground walnuts (5 ounces)
½ cup oatmeal (quick or old-fashioned)
¼ cup seedless raspberry preserves

Preheat the oven to 375° F. Spray the bottom and sides of an 8-inch layer pan with spray shortening, line the bottom of the pan with parchment or wax paper, and spray with more shortening.

In a large heavy saucepan, melt the butter, stirring occasionally. Remove from the heat.

Stir in the brown sugar, cinnamon, cloves, lemon peel, salt, cornstarch, ground walnuts, and oatmeal until a dry crumbly dough forms. Press about half the dough (about 1¼ cups) into the bottom of the pan to form a firm even layer. Spread the raspberry preserves evenly over the dough, leaving ½ inch of the edge uncovered. Crumble the remaining dough into small pieces and scatter them evenly over the top.

Bake until the top is light brown, about 30 minutes. Cool in the pan on a rack for 20 minutes. Run a knife around the edge of the cake, cover with wax paper, and invert onto a plate. Remove the pan and peel off the lining paper. Cover with a serving plate and invert. Remove the plate and wax paper and cool about 15 minutes.

Makes 8 servings

Toasted Coconut Torte

Toasting nuts before adding them to a batter crisps them and heightens their flavor. The only drawback is that toasting usually requires an additional cooking step and an extra pan. Not here. In this recipe, shredded coconut toasts right in the saucepan while the butter melts. Then it's made like any one-pot cake. The results are luscious, somewhere between a macaroon and white chocolate mousse.

¼ pound (1 stick) unsalted butter

2 cups unsweetened shredded coconut

4 ounces white chocolate, broken into
   pieces

½ cup sugar

3 eggs

¼ cup light rum

1 tablespoon dried orange peel

1 teaspoon vanilla extract

¼ cup cornstarch

½ teaspoon baking powder

Preheat the oven to 375° F. Spray the bottom and sides of an 8-inch layer pan with spray shortening, line the bottom of the pan with parchment or wax paper, and spray with more shortening.

In a large heavy saucepan over medium heat, begin melting the butter. Add the coconut and stir until lightly browned, about 1 minute. Remove from the heat, add the chocolate, and stir until completely melted.

Mix in the sugar. Mix in the eggs, rum, orange peel, vanilla, and cornstarch. Add the baking powder in pinches to remove any lumps and stir thoroughly into the batter.

Pour and scrape the batter into the pan and bake for 25 minutes, or until a tester inserted in the center of the cake comes out with a damp crumb clinging to it. Cool in the pan on a rack for 20 minutes. Run a knife around the edge of the cake, cover with wax paper, and invert onto a plate. Remove the pan and peel off the lining paper. Cover with a rack and invert. Remove the plate and wax paper and cool about 15 minutes more.

Makes 10 servings

NOTE: Top with French Chocolate Glaze (page 100) and you'll have a dessert that's closer to candy than cake.

Perfectly Plain Cheesecake

There is no cake simpler or more luxurious than an unadorned cheesecake. This recipe is a gem. Its results are elegant —silken smooth and custard soft.

2 pounds cream cheese, at room
   temperature
1 cup sugar
2 tablespoons vanilla extract

¼ cup brandy
5 eggs
¾ cup graham cracker or cookie crumbs

Preheat the oven to 350° F. Spray the inside of a 2-quart soufflé dish or a 9-inch cheesecake pan with vegetable oil spray and dust with the graham cracker or cookie crumbs.

In a large bowl, mix the cream cheese and sugar with a large wooden spoon until smooth and soft. Mix in the vanilla, brandy, and eggs until the batter is well blended.

Pour the batter into the dish or pan and bake for 1½ hours, or until the center feels barely firm to the touch. Turn off the oven, open the oven door, and cool the cake in the oven for 30 minutes.

Remove the cake to a rack and cool in the pan for 1 hour more, until the pan is cool enough to handle. Cover with a sheet of plastic wrap or wax paper and a plate. Invert. Remove the pan and refrigerate, upside down, for 1 hour. Place a serving plate over the cheesecake and invert. Remove the top plate and the plastic wrap or wax paper. Refrigerate until chilled through, at least 1 hour more.

Makes 16 servings

NOTE: This cheesecake may also be made following the method described on page 49.

Cognac Pumpkin Cheesecake

Pumpkin cheesecake is often overwhelmed by the cinnamon, ginger, and nutmeg triumvirate, but here, the spices are gently in the background, allowing the pumpkin and cognac to shine through.

¾ cup graham cracker or cookie crumbs

2 pounds cream cheese, at room temperature

1½ cups sugar

2 tablespoons cornstarch

½ teaspoon ground ginger

1 teaspoon ground cinnamon

⅛ teaspoon grated nutmeg

Pinch of ground cloves (optional)

1 can (1 pound) pumpkin puree

¼ cup cognac or brandy

5 eggs

Preheat the oven to 350° F. Spray the inside of a 2-quart soufflé dish or a 9-inch cheesecake pan with vegetable oil spray and dust with the graham cracker crumbs.

In a large bowl, mix the cream cheese and the sugar with a large wooden spoon until smooth and soft. Mix in the cornstarch, ginger, cinnamon, nutmeg, and clove, if using. Mix in the pumpkin puree, cognac, and eggs until the batter is well blended.

Pour the batter into the dish or pan and bake for 1 hour and 45 minutes, or until the center feels firm to the touch. Turn off the oven, open the oven door, and cool the cake in the oven for 30 minutes.

Remove the cake to a rack and cool in the pan for 1 hour more, until the pan is cool enough to handle. Cover with a sheet of plastic wrap or wax paper and a plate. Invert. Remove the pan and refrigerate, upside down, for 1 hour. Place a serving plate over the cheesecake and invert. Remove the top plate and the plastic wrap or wax paper. Refrigerate until chilled through, at least 1 hour more. Cut with a long sharp knife dipped in warm water.

Makes 16 servings

NOTE: This cheesecake may also be made following the method described on page 49.

Cannoli Cheese Torte

This ricotta and cream cheese cake recalls the Old World flavor of cannoli brimming with ricotta cream, chocolate, and dried fruit. As a cheesecake, this version has been slimmed down with light cream cheese and skim-milk ricotta.

24 chocolate wafers
1 pound reduced-fat cream cheese, at
  room temperature
16 ounces part-skim ricotta cheese
1 cup sugar

1 tablespoon vanilla extract
¼ cup dark rum
Pinch of salt
5 eggs
1 cup raisins

Preheat the oven to 300° F. Grease the inside of a 2-quart soufflé dish or a 9-inch cheesecake pan with vegetable oil spray. Crumble four of the chocolate wafers into crumbs and dust the greased dish with them.

In a large bowl, beat the cream cheese and ricotta cheese with a large wooden spoon until soft and smooth. Mix in the sugar, vanilla, rum, and salt. Beat in the eggs until the batter is smooth. Break the remaining chocolate wafers into small pieces and mix them into the batter along with the raisins.

Pour the batter into the dish or pan and place it in a larger pan filled with water. Bake for 2½ hours, or until the top is brown and a tester inserted into a crack in the top comes out almost clean. Turn off the oven, open the oven door, and cool the cake in the oven for 30 minutes.

Remove to a rack and cool in the pan for 1 hour more, until the pan is cool enough to handle. Cover with a sheet of plastic wrap or wax paper and an inverted plate. Invert. Remove the pan and refrigerate, upside down, for 1 hour. Place a serving plate over the cheesecake and invert. Remove the top plate and the plastic wrap or wax paper. Refrigerate until chilled through, at least 1 hour more. Cut with a long sharp knife dipped in warm water.

Makes 16 servings

FRUIT AND VEGETABLE
CAKES

Quick Carrot Cake

Cherry Yogurt Cake

Brandy-Applesauce Spice Cake

Dark Dark Fruitcake

"German" Chocolate Cake

Pumpkin Bundt Cake

Rummy Pineapple Cake

Apricot-Cardamom Tea Cake

Maple Banana Cake

Quick Jewish Apple Cake

When they first appeared in the mid-1960s, vegetable cakes, such as carrot cake and pumpkin bread, seemed to be a new breed of so-called health food. Carrot cake, too good to be good for you, fast became the stealth bomber of vegetables, claiming to deliver all the nutrition of fresh carrots under the sweet disguise of dessert. It was supposed to be guiltless goo, packed with vitamins, but its actual nutrition value was closer to that of the miniature marzipan carrots sprouting across the frosting than to the real produce in its batter.

Vegetable and fruit cakes *do* have their redeeming healthful qualities. Unlike other confections, they contain some dietary fiber and a modicum of vitamins. Most call for oil, rather than butter, a change that does decrease the level of saturated fat and cholesterol in the cake. But all that goodness comes packaged with a mountain of calories. A typical four-ounce wedge of carrot cake has the same four hundred calories as any slice of cake, along with hefty amounts of fat, sugar, and sodium.

So if it isn't good for you, why bother? Vegetables certainly don't make a cake taste any better. In fact, they don't add flavor at all. Who could honestly say that the sugar and spice of a carrot cake has anything to do with the flavor of a carrot?

The only discernible virtue that a vegetable or fruit brings to a cake is moisture—

rich, stick-to-your-fork dampness that doesn't last for just a day or two. It's moisture that keeps coming and coming, maintaining the velvety crumb of the cake for a week or more.

It's all from the water in the vegetable or fruit. During baking, some liquid is leached out into the batter, helping the cake crumbs to swell and soften as they set. But the real magic happens after the cake has cooled. It is then that the sugar in the cake continues, slowly and steadily, to attract water, out of the shreds of produce and into the batter, permeating the body of the cake with liquid. Because sugar absorbs moisture for as long as it can from wherever it can, vegetable and fruit cakes are guaranteed to stay moist until the last crumb.

Quick Carrot Cake

This carrot cake has the dense, moist interior and extended shelf life of recipes that take twice as long to prepare. Starting with the eggs and incorporating the oil in a slow, steady stream creates a thick emulsion that keeps this cake from getting overly oily, a common problem in other carrot cakes.

2 eggs	1 teaspoon baking soda
¾ cup sugar	1 cup flour
¾ cup vegetable oil	3 cups shredded carrots (or 4 carrots,
1 teaspoon vanilla extract	peeled and shredded)
2 teaspoons ground cinnamon	1 cup walnut pieces
¼ teaspoon salt	

Preheat the oven to 350° F. Grease and flour an 8-inch layer pan.

In a large mixing bowl, beat the eggs with a fork until well blended. Mix in the sugar. Add the oil in a steady stream, mixing all the while, until the mixture is thick and smooth. Mix in the vanilla, cinnamon, and salt. Add the baking soda in pinches, breaking up any lumps with your fingers. Stir in thoroughly. Stir in the flour, shredded carrots, and walnut pieces, just until blended.

Pour and scrape the batter into the pan and bake for 40 to 45 minutes, or until a tester inserted in the center comes out clean. Cool in the pan on a rack for 10 minutes. Remove from the pan and cool on the rack for about 15 minutes more.

Makes 8 servings

NOTE: Top this with White Chocolate–Cream Cheese Icing (page 99) or Brandy Cream Cheese Icing (page 97), if desired, or make 2 cakes and layer them with icing for a full-blown extravagance.

Cherry Yogurt Cake

Yogurt is the secret behind this cake's melt-in-your-mouth tenderness. Its flavor comes from two sources—the cherry preserves in the bottom of the container of cherry yogurt and a handful of dried cherries. Make sure you use dried cherries that are labeled either "red" or "sour." This is the only variety that has the tartness and bright fruitiness to stand out in a cake. Dried cherries are available in specialty food shops and many supermarkets.

¼ pound (1 stick) unsalted butter

1 cup sugar

Pinch of salt

1 teaspoon vanilla extract

1 cup lowfat cherry yogurt

2 eggs

1 teaspoon baking soda

2 cups flour

1 cup dried cherries

Preheat the oven to 350° F. Grease and flour an 8-inch layer pan.

In a large heavy saucepan over medium heat, melt the butter, stirring occasionally. Remove from the heat.

Stir in the sugar, salt, vanilla, yogurt, and eggs. Add the baking soda in pinches, breaking up any lumps with your fingers. Stir in thoroughly. Stir in the flour and cherries, just until blended.

Pour and scrape the batter into the pan and bake for 50 to 55 minutes, or until a tester inserted in the center comes out clean. Cool in the pan on a rack for 10 minutes. Remove from the pan and cool on the rack for about 15 minutes more.

Makes 8 servings

NOTE: If you wish, ice this cake with White Chocolate–Cream Cheese Icing (page 99).

Brandy-Applesauce Spice Cake

This cake will stay moist and fresh-tasting for a week or more. Its stamina comes from an extra-large scoop of applesauce, its spicy and sophisticated flavor from a pungent blend of spices and a jolt of brandy.

¼ pound (1 stick) unsalted butter
1 cup sugar
1½ cups applesauce
⅛ teaspoon ground allspice
2 teaspoons ground cinnamon
1 teaspoon ground ginger

1 teaspoon vanilla extract
2 tablespoons brandy
2 eggs
2 teaspoons baking soda
2 cups flour
1 cup raisins

Preheat the oven to 375° F. Grease and flour a 9-inch square baking pan.

In a large heavy saucepan over medium heat, melt the butter, stirring occasionally. Remove from the heat.

Stir in the sugar, applesauce, allspice, cinnamon, ginger, vanilla, brandy, and eggs. Add the baking soda in pinches, breaking up any lumps with your fingers. Stir in thoroughly. Stir in the flour and raisins, just until blended.

Pour and scrape the batter into the pan and bake for 45 minutes, or until a tester inserted in the center comes out clean. Cool in the pan on a rack for 10 minutes. Remove from the pan and cool on the rack for about 15 minutes more.

Makes 9 to 12 servings

NOTE: This cake is great just as it is, but it can be dusted with confectioners' sugar or slathered with Rummy Maple Icing (page 101).

Dark Dark Fruitcake

The deep mahogany color of the batter is reinforced on four fronts—with dark brown sugar, dark molasses, cinnamon, and black coffee. The intensity of the color is matched by an equally potent blend of flavors. Citrus, spices, molasses, coffee, dried fruit, and nuts blend and strengthen one another to create a sum infinitely greater than its parts.

4 tablespoons (½ stick) unsalted butter
¼ cup (packed) dark brown sugar
½ cup dark molasses
1 tablespoon dried lemon peel
2 teaspoons ground ginger
1 teaspoon ground cinnamon
¼ teaspoon ground allspice
2 tablespoons instant-coffee powder

2 eggs
1 teaspoon baking soda
1 cup plus 2 tablespoons flour
½ cup very hot water
1 cup mixed dried fruit pieces
1 cup raisins
1 cup walnut or pecan pieces

Preheat the oven to 350° F. Grease and flour an 8-inch layer pan.

In a large heavy saucepan over medium heat, melt the butter, stirring occasionally. Remove from the heat.

Stir in the brown sugar, molasses, lemon peel, ginger, cinnamon, allspice, coffee powder, and eggs. Add the baking soda in pinches, breaking up any lumps with your fingers. Stir in thoroughly. Stir in the flour, just until blended. Add the hot water to the batter. Mix until smooth. Stir in the dried fruits, raisins, and nuts.

Pour and scrape the batter into the pan and bake for 45 to 50 minutes, or until a tester inserted in the center comes out clean. Cool in the pan on a rack for 10 minutes. Remove from the pan and cool on the rack for about 15 minutes more.

Makes 8 servings

"German" Chocolate Cake

Unlike the famous German's Sweet Chocolate Cake, which gets its title from the chocolate company that invented the recipe, this similarly named cake has been christened for the strange Teutonic addition of sauerkraut. Don't panic. As I mentioned earlier, the flavor of a vegetable has nothing to do with the flavor of the cake. The sauerkraut is more textural than anything. And talk about moist—*nothing* could make this cake go stale.

6 tablespoons (¾ stick) unsalted butter

¾ cup sugar

6 tablespoons cocoa powder

2 teaspoons vanilla extract

2 eggs

1 cup drained canned sauerkraut, rinsed and squeezed dry

Pinch of salt

½ teaspoon baking soda

½ teaspoon baking powder

½ cup water

1 cup flour

Preheat the oven to 350° F. Grease and flour an 8-inch layer pan.

In a large heavy saucepan over medium heat, melt the butter, stirring occasionally. Remove from the heat. Stir in the sugar, cocoa, vanilla, eggs, sauerkraut, and salt. Add the baking soda and baking powder in pinches, breaking up any lumps with your fingers. Stir in thorougly. Stir in the water, followed by the flour, just until blended.

Pour and scrape the batter into the pan and bake for 25 minutes, or until a tester inserted in the center comes out clean. Cool in the pan on a rack for 10 minutes. Remove from the pan and cool on the rack for 15 minutes more.

Makes 8 servings

NOTE: If you're feeling excessive, frost this with Chocolate Sour Cream Icing (page 97).

Pumpkin Bundt Cake

Whole wheat flour adds more than just nutrition to this autumnal cake. Its nutty flavor is the perfect background for the rustic flavor and meaty texture of pureed pumpkin. The batter is similar to that of a carrot cake with canned pumpkin puree taking the place of the carrots.

4 eggs

2 cups sugar

1¼ cups vegetable oil

1 can (1 pound) pumpkin puree

1 teaspoon vanilla extract

2 teaspoons ground cinnamon

⅛ teaspoon ground cloves or allspice

¼ teaspoon salt

2 teaspoons baking soda

2 teaspoons baking powder

1½ cups whole wheat flour

1½ cups all-purpose flour

1½ cups walnut pieces

Preheat the oven to 350° F. Grease and flour a 10-inch bundt pan.

In a large mixing bowl, mix the eggs with a large fork until well blended. Mix in the sugar. Add the oil in a steady stream, mixing all the while, until the mixture is thick and smooth. Mix in the pumpkin, vanilla, cinnamon, clove, and salt. Add the baking soda and baking powder in pinches, breaking up any lumps with your fingers. Stir in thoroughly. Stir in the whole wheat and all-purpose flours just until blended. Stir in the walnuts.

Pour and scrape the batter into the pan and bake for 45 to 50 minutes, or until a tester inserted in the center comes out clean. Cool in the pan on a rack for 10 minutes. Invert, remove the pan, and cool on the rack for about 15 minutes more.

Makes 10 to 12 servings

NOTE: This cake needs no icing, although it goes well with Coffee Icing (page 98). Add an extra teaspoon or two of water to the icing recipe to thin the icing slightly and help it trickle attractively down the ridges of the cake. Or top each slice with a dollop of Chestnut Buttercream (page 102).

Rummy Pineapple Cake

This cake is dense with fruit and an exotic tropical flavor from the combination of rum, ginger, and pineapple. During baking, the pineapple settles near the bottom. That makes the finished cake reminiscent of pineapple upside-down cake, only easier.

2 eggs
¾ cup (packed) dark brown sugar
¾ cup vegetable oil
1 teaspoon rum extract
1 teaspoon vanilla extract
½ teaspoon ground ginger

2 teaspoons dried lemon peel
¼ teaspoon salt
1 teaspoon baking soda
1¼ cups flour
1 can (20 ounces) crushed pineapple, drained (about 2 cups)

Preheat the oven to 350° F. Grease and flour an 8-inch layer pan.

In a large mixing bowl, mix the eggs with a large fork until well blended. Mix in the brown sugar. Add the oil in a steady stream, mixing all the while, until the mixture is thick and smooth. Mix in the rum extract, vanilla, ginger, lemon peel, and salt. Add the baking soda in pinches, breaking up any lumps with your fingers. Stir in thoroughly. Stir in the flour, just until blended. Stir in the pineapple.

Pour and scrape the batter into the pan and bake for 40 to 45 minutes, or until a tester inserted in the center comes out clean. Cool in the pan on a rack for 10 minutes. Remove from the pan and cool on the rack for about 15 minutes more.

Makes 8 servings

NOTE: This goes well with Lemon Icing (page 102). Or dust the top with confectioners' sugar, if you want.

Apricot-Cardamom Tea Cake

This aromatic tea cake is scented with cardamom. You might recognize its lightly floral ginger-scented fragrance from Danish pastry or Swedish coffee cake. The cake is given a subtle crunch by using ground almonds in place of some of the flour.

½ pound (2 sticks) unsalted butter

1 can (12 ounces) apricot filling

1 cup sugar

2 teaspoons vanilla extract

2 teaspoons ground cardamom

1 teaspoon dried lemon peel

3 tablespoons lemon juice

3 eggs

2 teaspoons baking powder

1 teaspoon baking soda

2 cups flour

1 cup ground almonds (about 5 ounces)

Preheat the oven to 350° F. Grease and flour a 10-inch bundt pan.

In a large heavy saucepan over medium heat, melt the butter, stirring occasionally. Remove from the heat.

Stir in the apricot filling, sugar, vanilla, cardamom, lemon peel, lemon juice, and eggs. Add the baking powder and baking soda in pinches, breaking up any lumps with your fingers. Stir in thoroughly. Stir in the flour and ground almonds, just until well blended.

Pour and scrape the batter into the pan and bake for 45 to 50 minutes, or until a tester inserted in the center comes out clean. Cool in the pan on a rack for 10 minutes. Invert, remove the pan, and cool on the rack for about 15 minutes more.

Makes 12 servings

NOTE: If you would like to ice this cake, try Lemon Icing (page 102), adding an extra teaspoon or two of lemon juice to the icing recipe to thin the icing slightly and help it trickle attractively down the ridges of the cake.

Maple Banana Cake

This is an exceptional cake, possessing the moist crumb and long storage capacity typical of banana cakes but without any overt banana flavor. Rather, it is the fragrance of maple that permeates the loaf, supported by a subtle undercurrent of fruit.

2 very ripe bananas
2 eggs
⅔ cup (packed) dark brown sugar
⅓ cup vegetable oil
⅔ cup maple syrup
1 teaspoon vanilla extract

½ teaspoon ground cinnamon
1 teaspoon baking soda
1 teaspoon baking powder
2¼ cups flour
⅔ cup tea (bottled or home-brewed)

Preheat the oven to 350° F. Grease and flour a 9-inch loaf pan.

In a large bowl, mash the bananas with the back of a fork. Add the eggs and brown sugar and mix until well blended. Add the oil in a steady stream, mixing all the while, until the mixture is thick and smooth. Mix in the maple syrup, vanilla, and cinnamon. Add the baking soda and baking powder in pinches, breaking up any lumps with your fingers. Stir in thoroughly. Stir in the flour, just until blended. Stir in the tea.

Pour and scrape the batter into the pan and bake for 1 hour, or until a tester inserted in the center comes out with just a crumb clinging to it. Cool in the pan on a rack for 10 minutes. Remove from the pan and cool on the rack for about 15 minutes more.

Makes 8 to 10 servings

NOTE: This cake is perfect unadorned, though it can be gilded with Rummy Maple Icing (page 101), if you want.

Quick Jewish Apple Cake

I have no idea what makes this apple cake Jewish, although I suspect it's the absence of milk or sour cream in the recipe, making it permissible at a kosher table even after a meat meal. The preparation is kept simple by using canned sliced apples rather than peeling, coring, and slicing apples by hand.

4 eggs

2 cups sugar

1 cup vegetable oil

½ cup orange juice

2 teaspoons vanilla extract

¼ teaspoon salt

1 tablespoon baking powder

3 cups flour

1 can (20 ounces) sliced apples, drained

1 teaspoon ground cinnamon

Preheat the oven to 350° F. Grease a 10-inch tube pan.

In a large mixing bowl, mix the eggs with a large fork until well blended. Mix in 1½ cups of the sugar. Add the oil in a steady stream, mixing all the while, until the mixture is thick and smooth. Mix in the orange juice, vanilla, and salt. Add the baking powder in pinches, breaking up any lumps with your fingers. Stir in thoroughly. Stir in the flour, just until blended.

Pour and scrape half the batter into the pan. Scatter half the apples on top and sprinkle with ¼ cup of the remaining sugar and ½ teaspoon of the cinnamon. Pour in the rest of the batter. Scatter the rest of the apples on top and sprinkle with the remaining sugar and remaining cinnamon. Bake for 50 to 55 minutes, or until a tester inserted in the center comes out with just a crumb clinging to it. Cool in the pan on a rack for 10 minutes. Remove from the pan and cool on the rack for about 15 minutes more.

Makes 10 to 12 servings

SHEET CAKES

Not-Too-Sweet Chocolate Sheet Cake

Lotsa Lemon Cake

Amaretto Almond Cake

The Easiest Best Brownies Ever

Raspberry Brownies

Granola Bars

Chocolate Chocolate-Chip Bars

Chocolate Oatmeal Chews

Sesame Squares

Cherry Crumbles

Cakes are meant to be shared, but sometimes, when the hordes get huge, a single layer just can't cut it. That's when a sheet cake can turn ten minutes of mixing into manna for the masses.

But sheet cakes aren't just big—they're versatile. The same cake can be decorated for a large celebration, or left uniced and cut into squares to eat out of hand for an after-school snack. They can even be turned into cookies—bar cookies.

I have always found baking cookies tedious. It's the batches. They keep going and going, and you have to time them, and the timer always goes off at the wrong moment, and one batch always burns, and—There has to be a better way. Baking cookies as sheet cakes is that better way. It makes no difference whether you bake a dozen or a gross, there's only one batch.

Not only are bar cookies really sheet cakes, so are fudge squares, shortbreads, and brownies. What is a brownie, after all, but a rich, dense sheet cake, cut into individual squares? And once you understand that, a whole world of oatmeal chews, chocolate chip shortbread, granola bars, and fruit-filled pastries falls instantly into your grasp.

Almost anything can be baked into a sheet cake: pound cake, butter cake, sponge cake, or pastry. Shortbread dough can be pushed into a rimmed pan to make a drove of bite-size buttery cookies and streusel crumbs packed into a tight layer will bake into a solid base for rich fruit- or nut-filled bars.

Unlike the other recipes in this book, all but one of the following cakes yield several dozen servings. If you're left with more than you can use, any of these cakes can be frozen without compromising flavor or consistency. To help protect them during freezing and to make them easier to use from the freezer, I usually wrap pairs of cake squares, brownies, or bar cookies in plastic wrap and then enclose a few together in a small foil package. That way, I can remove the number of packages I need when I need them, have them defrosted in minutes, and never have to deal with a second generation of leftovers.

Not-Too-Sweet Chocolate Sheet Cake

This is the perfect all-purpose chocolate cake for feeding a crowd. Feel free to used a reduced-fat product, but don't use fat-*free* sour cream or the cake will be dense and rubbery.

12 tablespoons (1½ sticks) unsalted butter

6 ounces unsweetened chocolate, broken into pieces

1 box (1 pound) dark brown sugar

1 tablespoon vanilla extract

2 cups sour cream, regular or reduced-fat

4 eggs

2 teaspoons baking soda

2 cups plus 2 tablespoons flour

Preheat the oven to 350° F. Grease and flour a 9 x 13 x 2-inch baking pan.

In a large heavy saucepan over medium heat, begin melting the butter. When it's about half melted, add the chocolate and stir until the chocolate is about half melted. Remove from the heat and continue stirring until the butter and chocolate are fully melted.

Stir in the brown sugar, vanilla, sour cream, and eggs. Add the baking soda in pinches, breaking up any lumps with your fingers. Stir thoroughly. Stir in the flour, just until well blended.

Pour and scrape the batter into the pan. Spread evenly and smooth the top. Bake for 25 to 30 minutes, or until the cake is set and a tester inserted in the center comes out with just a crumb clinging to it. Remove from the oven and cool on a rack for 15 minutes. Remove the pan and invert onto a rack. Cool on the rack to room temperature. Cut into 24 squares.

Makes 24 servings

NOTE: This cake can be iced with a double batch of Chocolate Sour Cream Icing (page 97), Chocolate Cream Cheese Icing (page 98), White Chocolate–Cream Cheese Icing (page 99), or Chocolate Mint Icing (page 99).

Lotsa Lemon Cake

This fragrant butter cake is mildly perfumed with lemon. This cake was tested with both fresh and bottled lemon juice. Although the flavor of the cake was fuller and more intense with fresh juice, the bottled juice gave perfectly fine results.

½ pound (2 sticks) unsalted butter

2 tablespoons dried lemon peel

2 cups sugar

3 tablespoons lemon juice, fresh or bottled

Pinch of salt

4 eggs

2 teaspoons baking powder

1 teaspoon baking soda

3 cups flour

1 cup milk

Preheat the oven to 350° F. Grease and flour a 9 × 13 × 2-inch baking pan.

In a large heavy saucepan over medium heat, begin melting the butter. When it's about half melted, remove from the heat, add the lemon peel, and stir until the butter is completely melted.

Stir in the sugar, lemon juice, salt, and eggs. Add the baking powder and baking soda in pinches, breaking up any lumps with your fingers. Stir thoroughly. The mixture will foam up. Before it foams too much, stir in the flour, just until well blended. Stir in the milk until smooth.

Pour and scrape the batter into the pan. Spread evenly and smooth the top. Bake for 25 to 30 minutes, or until the cake is set and a tester inserted in the center comes out with just a crumb clinging to it. Remove from the oven and cool on a rack for 15 minutes. Remove from the pan, invert back onto the rack, and cool to room temperature. Cut into 24 squares.

Makes 24 servings

NOTE: Frost this cake with a double batch of Lemon Icing (page 102), sieve confectioners' sugar over the top, or top each piece with a dollop of whipped cream.

Amaretto Almond Cake

This cake is heady with nuts and a triple rich almond flavor. First the butter and sugar are mixed with almond pastry filling, a mixture of ground nuts, nut extracts, and sweeteners. Then almond liqueur is added. Finally, ground almonds are substituted for almost half the flour. Serve on a winter evening with butter almond ice cream or a chocolate sauce.

½ pound (2 sticks) unsalted butter

1 cup sugar

1 can (12½ ounces) almond filling

1 teaspoon vanilla extract

¼ cup amaretto

4 eggs

1 tablespoon baking powder

1½ cups ground almonds

2 cups flour

Preheat the oven to 350° F. Grease and flour a 9 × 13 × 2-inch baking pan.

In a large heavy saucepan over medium heat, begin melting the butter. When it's about half melted, remove from the heat and stir until fully melted.

Stir in the sugar, almond filling, vanilla, amaretto, and eggs. Add the baking powder in pinches, breaking up any lumps with your fingers. Stir thoroughly. Stir in the ground almonds and the flour, just until well blended.

Pour and scrape the batter into the pan. Spread evenly and smooth the top. Bake for 25 minutes, or until the cake is set and a tester inserted in the center comes out with just a crumb clinging to it. Remove from the oven and cool on a rack for 15 minutes. Remove from the pan, invert back onto the rack, and cool to room temperature. Cut into 24 squares.

Makes 24 servings

NOTE: Chestnut Buttercream (page 102) gilds this cake in a most sophisticated way.

The Easiest Best Brownies Ever

The title of this recipe says it all.

½ pound (2 sticks) unsalted butter
6 ounces unsweetened chocolate, broken
   into pieces
1 teaspoon vanilla extract

2½ cups sugar
5 eggs
2 cups flour
2 cups walnut pieces

Preheat the oven to 350° F. Line a 10 × 15 × 1-inch jelly-roll pan with foil. Grease the foil.

In a large heavy saucepan over medium heat, begin melting the butter. When it's about half melted, add the chocolate. When the chocolate is half melted, remove from the heat and stir until the butter and chocolate are completely melted.

Stir in the vanilla, sugar, eggs, and flour, stirring until the batter is smooth. Stir in the walnuts.

Pour and scrape the batter into the pan and smooth the top. The batter will nearly fill the pan. Bake for 25 minutes, or until the cake is just set. Remove from the oven and cool on a rack for 10 minutes. Invert onto a baking sheet, remove the foil, and invert back onto the rack. Cool to room temperature. Cut with a serrated knife into 48 bars.

Makes 24 servings

Raspberry Brownies

These brownies are outrageously rich. An extra-large addition of chocolate and a can of raspberry pastry filling take the place of the usual butter. Because the chocolate is melted without the protection of some butter in the pot, it is essential to use a heavy saucepan and cook over the lowest possible heat to prevent the chocolate from scorching. Stir it the whole time it is over the heat, and remove it from the heat when it's about half melted, allowing it to finish melting by residual heat.

½ pound unsweetened chocolate, broken into pieces

1 can (12 ounces) raspberry filling

2 cups sugar

¼ teaspoon salt

3 eggs

1 tablespoon vanilla extract

2 cups flour

2 cups walnut or pecan pieces

Preheat the oven to 350° F. Line a 9 × 13 × 2-inch baking pan with foil. Grease the foil.

In a large heavy saucepan over low heat, begin melting the chocolate, stirring constantly. When it's half melted, remove from heat and continue stirring until it's completely melted.

Stir in the raspberry filling, sugar, salt, eggs, and vanilla. Stir in the flour, just until smooth. Stir in the walnuts.

Pour and scrape the batter into the pan and spread evenly. Bake for 25 minutes, or until a tester inserted in the center comes out with a damp crumb clinging to it. Cool on a rack for 10 minutes. Invert onto a baking sheet, remove the foil, and invert back onto the rack. Cool to room temperature. Cut with a serrated knife into 30 pieces.

Makes 15 servings

Granola Bars

The nut-and-honey flavor of granola cereal is intensified by peanut butter and molasses-rich brown sugar in these extra-chewy brownie bars. They're chock full of fruit, nuts, and grain and can be taken over the top by adding chocolate chips.

¼ pound (1 stick) unsalted butter
¼ cup peanut butter
1 cup (packed) light or dark brown sugar
1 cup granulated sugar
2 eggs
2 teaspoons vanilla extract

½ teaspoon ground cinnamon
2 teaspoons baking soda
2 cups flour
2 cups granola, any variety
1 cup semisweet chocolate chips
 (optional)

Preheat the oven to 400° F. Grease a 10 × 15 × 1-inch jelly-roll pan.

In a large heavy saucepan over medium heat, begin melting the butter. When it's about half melted, add the peanut butter and stir until the peanut butter is almost melted. Remove from the heat and continue stirring until the butter and peanut butter are completely melted.

Stir in the brown sugar, granulated sugar, eggs, vanilla, and cinnamon. Add the baking soda in pinches, breaking up any lumps with your fingers. Stir thoroughly. Stir in the flour, just until well blended. Stir in the granola and the chocolate chips, if using.

Pour and scrape the batter into the pan. Spread evenly and smooth the top. Bake for 22 minutes, or until the cake is just set. Remove from the oven and let cool on a rack for 10 minutes. Leave the cake in the pan and cut into 60 pieces, each about 1½ inches square.

Makes 30 servings

Chocolate Chocolate-Chip Bars

There may be no way to improve upon a chocolate chip cookie, but this recipe tries by lacing the batter with cocoa. The effect is to blur the distinctions between cookie and brownie. The chocolate chips become an extension of the cake itself. The recipe calls for equal parts brown and white sugar. For an even richer taste, use all brown sugar.

½ pound (2 sticks) unsalted butter

3 tablespoons cocoa powder

¾ cup dark brown sugar

¾ cup granulated sugar

1 teaspoon vanilla extract

2 eggs

1 teaspoon baking soda

2¼ cups flour

2 cups semisweet chocolate chips

Preheat the oven to 375° F. Grease a 10 × 15 × 1-inch jelly-roll pan.

In a large heavy saucepan over medium heat, begin melting the butter. When it's about half melted, remove from the heat and stir until the butter is completely melted.

Stir in the cocoa powder, brown sugar, granulated sugar, vanilla, and eggs. Add the baking soda in pinches, breaking up any lumps with your fingers. Stir thoroughly. Stir in the flour, just until well blended. Stir in the chocolate chips.

Pour and scrape the batter into the pan. Spread evenly and smooth the top. Bake for 23 minutes, or until the cake is just set. Remove from the oven and cool on a rack for 10 minutes. Leave the cake in the pan and cut into 60 pieces, each about 1½ inches square.

Makes 30 servings

Chocolate Oatmeal Chews

Although indulgence and health are too often mutually exclusive, one ingredient manages to close the gap with impeccable nutrition credentials and a chewy, crunchy charm. Oatmeal gives baked goods a provocative texture and innate chewiness. In this recipe, it's teamed with chocolate for richness and intense flavor.

1 pound (4 sticks) unsalted butter
2 ounces unsweetened chocolate, broken
   into pieces
1 cup (packed) dark brown sugar
1 cup granulated sugar
2 teaspoons vanilla extract

3 eggs
2 teaspoons baking soda
1½ cups flour
2 cups oatmeal (quick or old-fashioned)
1 cup semisweet chocolate chips

Preheat the oven to 375° F. Grease a 10 ×15 × 1-inch jelly-roll pan.

In a large heavy saucepan over medium heat, begin melting the butter. When it's about half melted, add the chocolate. Stir until the chocolate is half melted. Remove from the heat and stir until the butter and chocolate are completely melted.

Stir in the brown sugar, granulated sugar, vanilla, and eggs. Add the baking soda in pinches, breaking up any lumps with your fingers. Stir thoroughly. Stir in the flour, just until well blended. Stir in the oatmeal and chocolate chips.

Pour and scrape the batter into the pan. Spread evenly and smooth the top. Bake for 23 minutes, or until the cake is just set. Remove from the oven and let cool on a rack for 10 minutes. Leave the cake in the pan and cut into 60 pieces, each about 1½ inches square.

Makes 30 servings

Sesame Squares

Irrationally buttery, these tiny delicate squares are chockablock with toasted sesame seeds. Their incomparable sophistication belies the ease of preparation. Once the butter is melted, the other ingredients are added and combined into a stiff, pliable dough that is pushed into a pan and baked.

½ pound (2 sticks) unsalted butter

2 cups sesame seeds (see Note)

½ cup (packed) light brown sugar

1 teaspoon vanilla extract

2 cups flour

6 tablespoons cornstarch

Preheat the oven to 375° F.

In a large heavy saucepan over medium heat, begin melting the butter. When it's half melted, add the sesame seeds and stir until the butter is completely melted. Remove from the heat.

Stir in the brown sugar and vanilla. Add the flour and cornstarch and stir until a smooth, stiff dough forms, about 30 seconds.

Put the dough in a 10 × 15 × 1-inch jelly-roll pan and pat into an even layer. Bake for 20 minutes. Cool on a rack for 2 minutes. With a fork, mark off 32 pieces in a 4-by-8 pattern, making perforated lines that pierce through the cake. Let cool to room temperature. Cut along the perforated lines to separate into serving pieces.

Makes 32 pieces

NOTE: For this quantity of sesame seeds, you might want to go to a health-food store and buy them in bulk.

Cherry Crumbles

These impressive cake squares are effortless to make. A crumb mixture is pressed into a baking pan, topped with a can of cherry-pie filling, and finished with more crumbs. During baking, it all combines into a crunchy, gooey confection.

6 tablespoons (¾ stick) unsalted butter
6 tablespoons (packed) light brown sugar
Pinch of salt
1 cup plus 2 tablespoons flour

½ cup oatmeal (quick or old-fashioned)
1 tablespoon dried lemon peel
1 can (20 ounces) cherry pie filling

Preheat the oven to 375° F.

In a large heavy saucepan, melt the butter, stirring occasionally. Remove from the heat.

Stir in the sugar, salt, flour, oatmeal, and lemon peel until a dry crumbly dough forms. Press about two-thirds of the dough (about 1⅔ cups) into the bottom of a 9-inch square baking pan to make a firm even layer. Top with an even layer of the pie filling. Sprinkle the remaining dough evenly over the top.

Bake until lightly browned, about 30 minutes. Remove to a rack and cool for 20 minutes. Leave the cake in the pan and cut into 16 squares.

Makes 16 pieces

ICINGS ON THE CAKES

Chocolate Sour Cream Icing

Brandy Cream Cheese Icing

Coffee Icing

Chocolate Cream Cheese Icing

White Chocolate–Cream Cheese Icing

Chocolate Mint Icing

French Chocolate Glaze

Rummy Maple Icing

Lemon Icing

Chestnut Buttercream

Icings, by their nature, are much simpler than cakes. Most of them are mixed in a single bowl without much ado, so developing a series of one-pot icings is hardly novel. The icings here were not selected for how many bowls they use, but for their speed and ease. All of them can be mixed in minutes with a spoon and a pot or bowl, and all of them are ready to frost a cake in five minutes.

Chocolate Sour Cream Icing

6 ounces semisweet chocolate chips   ½ cup sour cream, regular or reduced-fat

Melt the chocolate chips in a bowl set over boiling water or in a microwave at full power for 45 seconds. Stir until smooth. Mix in the sour cream until smooth.

Makes about 1½ cups, or enough to generously ice a single cake layer

Brandy Cream Cheese Icing

8 ounces cream cheese or light cream
   cheese, at room temperature
2 tablespoons unsalted butter, softened
1 cup confectioners' sugar

1 tablespoon honey
1 teaspoon vanilla extract
2 tablespoons brandy

Beat the cream cheese and butter with a fork or whisk until smooth. Add the confectioners' sugar and mix until smooth and fluffy. Beat in the honey, vanilla, and brandy. If the icing is too thin, refrigerate to thicken.

Makes about 1½ cups, or enough to generously ice a single cake layer

Coffee Icing

2 tablespoons instant-coffee powder

1 tablespoon boiling water

1 teaspoon vanilla extract

2 tablespoons brandy

2 tablespoons unsalted butter, softened

8 ounces cream cheese or light cream cheese, at room temperature

1 cup confectioners' sugar

In a bowl, dissolve the coffee powder in the boiling water. Stir in the vanilla and brandy. Beat in the butter and cream cheese until smooth. If the icing is too thin, refrigerate to thicken.

Makes about 1½ cups, or enough to generously ice a single cake layer

Chocolate Cream Cheese Icing

1 tablespoon unsalted butter

2 ounces semisweet chocolate, broken into pieces

1 teaspoon vanilla extract

2 tablespoons rum or fruit liqueur

1 teaspoon instant-coffee powder

8 ounces cream cheese or light cream cheese, at room temperature

In a heavy-bottomed medium saucepan over medium heat, begin melting the butter. When the butter is half melted, add the chocolate and stir until the chocolate is half melted. Remove from the heat and stir until the butter and chocolate are melted. Stir in the vanilla, rum, and coffee powder. Beat in the cream cheese until smooth. If the icing is too thin, refrigerate to thicken.

Makes about 1½ cups, or enough to generously ice a single cake layer

White Chocolate–Cream Cheese Icing

4 tablespoons (½ stick) unsalted butter

3 ounces white chocolate, broken into pieces

8 ounces cream cheese or light cream cheese, at room temperature

1 teaspoon lemon juice

In a heavy-bottomed medium saucepan over medium heat, melt the butter. Remove from the heat and stir in the white chocolate, stirring until it melts. Beat in the cream cheese and lemon juice until smooth. If the icing is too thin, refrigerate to thicken.

Makes about 1½ cups, or enough to generously ice a single cake layer

Chocolate Mint Icing

6 ounces Peppermint Patties

2 to 3 tablespoons milk

Break the Peppermint Patties into a heavy-bottomed medium saucepan. Melt over low heat, stirring constantly. Mix in the milk until the icing is light and smooth.

Makes about 1 cup, or enough to ice a single cake layer

French Chocolate Glaze

4 tablespoons (½ stick) unsalted butter
1 tablespoon honey
2 ounces unsweetened chocolate, broken
   into pieces

2 ounces semisweet chocolate, broken into
   pieces

In a large heavy saucepan over medium heat, melt the butter with the honey, stirring frequently. Remove from the heat and add the chocolates. Stir until melted and completely smooth. Let stand until lightly thickened.

To glaze a cake, place a single layer on a rack set over a pan. Pour half the glaze over the top. Smooth around the sides with an icing spatula or knife. Pour the rest over the top and smooth the top. If the glaze should get too thick before you're done, warm it slightly over low heat and proceed.

With a large, wide spatula, transfer the cake to a serving plate.

Makes about 1 cup, or enough to glaze a single cake layer

Rummy Maple Icing

4 tablespoons (½ stick) unsalted butter,
  softened
1½ cups confectioners' sugar
2 tablespoons cornstarch

⅛ teaspoon salt
¼ cup maple syrup
2 teaspoons dark rum

In a large mixing bowl, mash the butter into the confectioners' sugar and cornstarch with the back of a large fork until the butter has been broken into small grains. Stir in the salt and maple syrup, stirring until the mixture is very thick. Stir in the rum until completely smooth.

Makes about 1 cup, or enough to ice a single cake layer

Lemon Icing

4 tablespoons (½ stick) unsalted butter,
   softened
2 cups confectioners' sugar

Pinch of salt
½ teaspoon lemon or orange extract
2 tablespoons lemon juice

In a large mixing bowl, mash the butter into the confectioners' sugar with the back of a large fork until the butter has been broken into small grains. Stir in the salt, extract, and lemon juice, stirring until the mixture is very thick and completely smooth.

Makes about 1 cup, or enough to ice a single cake layer

Chestnut Buttercream

¼ pound (1 stick) unsalted butter
1 cup canned chestnut puree
6 tablespoons confectioners' sugar

Pinch of salt
¼ teaspoon almond extract (optional)

In a large saucepan, melt the butter over medium heat. When it's half melted, remove the pan from the heat and mix in the chestnut puree with a large fork or small whisk. Stir in the confectioners' sugar, salt, and almond extract, if using, stirring until smooth and fluffy.

Makes about 1¼ cups, or enough to generously ice a single cake layer

INDEX